**EXTENDING
YOUR
HOUSE**

a Consumer Publication

Consumers' Association
publishers of **Which?**
14 Buckingham Street
London WC2N 6DS

a Consumer Publication

edited by Edith Rudinger

published by Consumers' Association
publishers of **Which?**

Consumer Publications are
available from Consumers'
Association, and from
booksellers.
Details of other
Consumer Publications
are given at the end of this
book.

© Consumers' Association 1971
amended reprints 1971, 1972, 1973
revised June 1974, February 1976
reprinted with minor revisions May 1977

ISBN 0 85202 116 X

 Computer typeset
and printed offset litho
by Page Bros (Norwich) Ltd.

CONTENTS

Foreword

First considerations   *page* 1

Planning the extension   19

The preparations   75

Prefabricated structures   100

Construction   104

Afterwards   127

Glossary   133

Index   148

This Consumer Publication was written and illustrated for the Consumers' Association by Ian Morris.
In the course of its preparation, CA consulted architects, surveyors, design consultants, builders, various professional bodies, civil servants and local authority officers.

Cover design by Peter Smith.

FOREWORD

This book is concerned with extending a house or a bungalow—not a flat, maisonette, or any building occupied by more
than one family.

The book suggests what you can do yourself towards planning
an extension, outlines the roles played by architects or other
specialists, and builders, describes the formalities that have to be
followed to obtain planning permission and other local authority
approvals, and summarises the way in which the design of an
extension is controlled by the Building Regulations.

Advice is not given on aesthetic points, but an extension, as well
as being big enough and well constructed, should give some visual
delight to owner, visitor and neighbour. No two extension
schemes are exactly the same, and it is impossible to be specific
about what should or should not be done in every situation, once
the statutory requirements have been met.

The book is not intended to replace the services of an architect
or similar consultant whose specialised knowledge will probably
be needed to a greater or less extent, depending on the size and
nature of the scheme.

If after reading the book you simply authorise an architect (or
perhaps a builder) to design and arrange for the construction of
your extension, you will at least know what is going on, even if you
yourself take no more active part in the operation. For the techni-
cally minded, there is a chapter on what happens during the
construction.

The book does not deal specifically with the building proce-
dures in Northern Ireland or in Scotland where the statutory
requirements are broadly similar to those in England and Wales
but the local government structure and many of the fittings and
methods of working in the building industry are different. Nor does
it deal in detail with extensions in the inner London area, where the
regulations about building work differ from those for the rest of the
country.

If you are intending to add to your home, first of all decide exactly what you would like to have. A finished extension is generally a compromise between what one would like to have and what one can afford, what one is allowed to have by law and how well the builder carries out one's wishes.

Points to bear in mind during the initial considerations include for what is the extra space wanted—extra bedroom? bathroom? studio? By whom will it be used, now and later—children? an old person? lodger? What would be the ideal size? Where should it be and what should it look like? Then you will have to determine your priorities, bearing in mind the site and the money available. Few people can say 'I want such-and-such and don't care how much it costs'. Most people have a limited amount to spend and want the best value for their money.

You should explore all the possible alternatives—whether to go upwards, sideways, forwards or to the rear, whether to build on or to convert—before settling on a particular scheme. For instance, do not decide to build a ground floor extension without consider-ing whether a loft conversion might not be more useful and economical. If a children's playroom is to be added to a bungalow, it may be possible for it to take the form of a ground floor extension approached from the sitting room, or it may be possible for it to be in the loft, approached by a staircase from either the hall or a child's bedroom. You may want to have the children going from their bedroom to their playroom without stampeding through your sitting room or, if the children are still very young, you may prefer to have the children playing on the ground floor where you can keep an eye on them. Also bear in mind that a children's playroom should have a use when the children no longer need it.

Some properties are restricted as far as their development is concerned by covenants in the title deeds, mostly laid down when the house was first built. A covenant may, for instance, stipulate that certain alterations or additions shall not be made or can be made only with the consent of the person who sold the land on which the property was built. Also, most mortgage deeds have a clause stipulating that the building society's approval must be obtained for any proposed alteration to the house.

First ideas may have to be modified and other possibilities explored before a decision is reached about the final scheme.

Putting ideas on paper

To clarify your own ideas, it is useful to make a sketch or sketches of alternative schemes. First measure all the relevant parts of the property and note the main features so that they can be indicated on a sketch plan to show the main points of your scheme.

The plan should be drawn to some sort of scale, showing everything in proportion: for instance, 1 mm representing 50 mm or 100 mm. Graph or squared paper can be helpful. Use a large enough sheet of paper to be able to show not only the proposed extension but also adjacent buildings or boundaries, and the whole of any rooms in the house which may be affected.

If the proposed extension is to be built on to an existing structure or will be close to the house or near the boundary of your property, do not just draw it as a rectangle in the middle of a sheet of paper. The sketch should show the position of the boundary and the side of the house.

walls

One of the basic rules is not to show walls simply as single lines. The main walls of a house are roughly the best part of a foot (300 mm) thick, and internal walls, those dividing one room from another, about 6 inches (150 mm). On a sketch to the scale of 1 : 100, these walls should therefore be indicated as 3 mm and 1·5 mm respectively. Proposed external and internal walls for the extension should be indicated in a similar way.

Indicate the exact positions of any door and window openings in the side wall and, if possible, show the whole of the rooms which are served by such doors and windows. If these rooms have doors and windows in other walls, show these too.

Show how the extension should link to the house itself. If the new part is to be approached through an existing door, this should be indicated. If part of an existing wall is to be demolished in order to join the extension to the house, show the wall to be removed as a dotted line and make a note on the sketch of any other obstructions, such as electric power points, central heating pipes or radiators, fixed to the wall which is to be removed. If the proposed scheme involves building on top of an existing structure, show the position and thickness of the walls of the existing structure.

drains
Many ground floor extensions and garages have to be constructed above or around existing drains. Drains should, therefore, be indicated particularly carefully on a sketch plan, differentiating where possible between the various types of pipes and drains.

The downpipes running from the roof gutter to ground level are rainwater pipes. It can be difficult to establish where the rainwater flows from there onwards.

Other types of pipes can be identified by tracing them to their sources, such as sink, bath and basins. Waste water from these is generally carried in $1\frac{1}{2}$ to 2-inch (about 50 mm) diameter vertical or inclined pipes outside the building, or shares the 4-inch (100 mm) diameter soil pipe leading from a lavatory. In houses built since 1966, soil pipes from lavatories are inside the building, usually boxed in by some removable covering, running vertically through the house. A 4-inch vertical pipe outside, running up to the top of the building, is for ventilation purposes. In older houses, the soil pipe from a lavatory comes through the external wall of the house and connects to the ventilation pipe outside.

It is also important to show inspection chambers, or manholes, on the sketch plan because these mark where drains change direction underground. You can tell an inspection chamber by its round or square metal cover set into the ground. If you take the cover off an inspection chamber, you may be able to see which

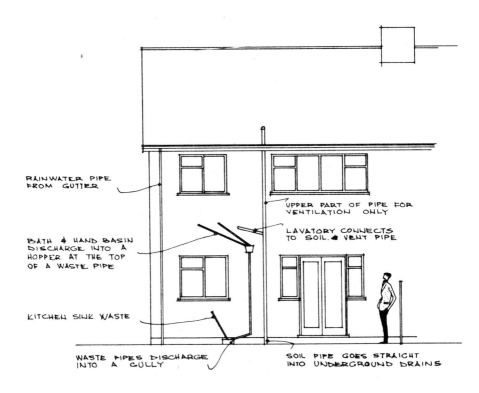

RAINWATER PIPE
FROM GUTTER

UPPER PART OF PIPE FOR
VENTILATION ONLY

BATH & HAND BASIN
DISCHARGE INTO A
HOPPER AT THE TOP
OF A WASTE PIPE

LAVATORY CONNECTS
TO SOIL & VENT PIPE

KITCHEN SINK WASTE

WASTE PIPES DISCHARGE
INTO A GULLY

SOIL PIPE GOES STRAIGHT
INTO UNDERGROUND DRAINS

pipes on a house built before 1966

drains run into it by turning likely taps or flushing the lavatory. In some cases, a rainwater pipe and a waste pipe from the house both discharge into the same chamber. The depth of an inspection chamber is important if new drains will have to connect into it. The depth is measured from the level of the edge of the ground to the lowest part of the open pipe which runs along the base.

On terraced houses, and on some other closely spaced properties, the drains from each property often run into a communal drain at the rear of the group of houses and then, at the end of the group, connect to the public sewer. But a detached or semi-detached house is more likely to have its own set of drains connected to the public sewer. Most local authorities keep plans which show the drains on properties in the district, and from one of these it should be possible to ascertain the direction of drains on a particular property and where they go. Public sewers come under the jurisdiction of the local authority, and building over them cannot be carried out without the agreement of the local authority. Where an extension would mean building over drains which are not in your ownership, you should in the first place contact the local authority for advice.

On the sketch plan you should indicate, as far as possible, the positions and sizes of all the vertical pipes, the positions of gullies, the positions, sizes and depths of inspection chambers, and where drains lie under the ground. If you know, show which of them take rainwater and which take waste water, and which lead from the lavatory.

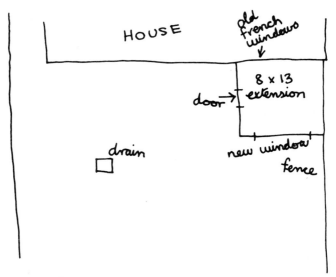

how not to draw a plan

SKETCH PLAN

the same drawing done properly

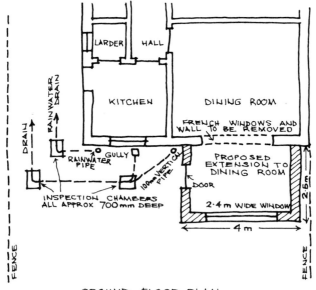

heights

If the extension is to be two storeys, draw a sketch plan for each floor.

It is useful to give a little more information by drawing a cross-section to indicate relative heights such as ceiling heights and window heights (and window sill levels on upper floors) and

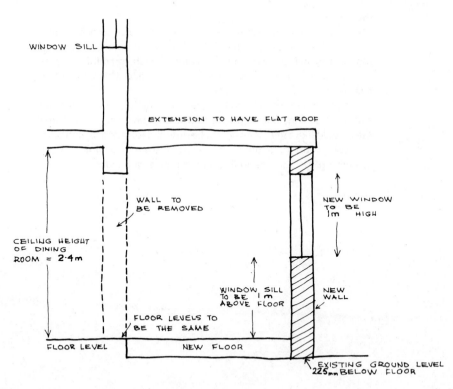

WINDOW SILL

EXTENSION TO HAVE FLAT ROOF

WALL TO
BE REMOVED

NEW WINDOW
TO BE
1m HIGH

CEILING HEIGHT
OF DINING
ROOM = 2·4m

WINDOW SILL
TO BE 1m
ABOVE FLOOR

NEW
WALL

FLOOR LEVELS TO
BE THE SAME

FLOOR LEVEL   NEW FLOOR

EXISTING GROUND LEVEL
225mm BELOW FLOOR

CROSS   SECTION
SCALE: 1mm   REPRESENTS   50mm

showing the difference between floor and ground levels. To find the difference between the existing floor level and the ground level, measure the distance between the window sill and the floor inside the room and the distance from the sill to the ground outside, and subtract one from the other. The scale of a cross-section should be not less than 1 : 50.

the sketch
Make sure that everything is labelled on the sketch plan and indicate the existing or intended use of all the rooms or parts of rooms shown. Put down any dimensions which you think could be important. And do not forget to state the scale to which the sketch has been drawn.

While it is not too difficult to make a sketch plan of part of an existing building, many people find it difficult to translate what they would like their extension to be, into the form of a sketch plan. But some sort of a drawing will be a useful document when discussing the scheme with an architect or a builder.

Professional advice

The title of 'architect' may be used only by a person who is a registered architect. Anyone calling himself an architect has to be registered with the Architects Registration Council of the United Kingdom and must have specific academic qualifications. He must adhere to a code of professional conduct, conditions of engagement and minimum scale of charges. Many architects are members of the Royal Institute of British Architects (RIBA).

There are also firms and individuals who carry out work similar to that of registered architects but who are not registered and are therefore prohibited from describing themselves as architects. An individual who is not registered as an architect carries on business under various titles such as architectural consultant or building design consultant or architectural surveyor. He is not forced to adhere to any professional codes, conditions or charges. No criterion for his degree of competence is laid down; his work could be anything from very good to completely useless.

Some local authorities keep in their offices a list of local architects for the public to consult, and registered architects in private practice are listed in the yellow pages of the telephone directory. An RIBA regional office can be asked to recommend architects in the area who would be suitable to carry out a particular project. Also the RIBA has a clients' advisory service in London.

Architects are not allowed by their code of professional conduct to advertise or solicit work. What they can do is to put up a display board with their name at the site where they are undertaking work. There is no such restriction on individuals who are not registered architects, and architectural consultants generally advertise in local newspapers. In the yellow pages of the telephone directory, they may be listed under 'building consultants' or 'design consultants'.

A building surveyor can be asked to perform a similar role to an architect—designing, preparing drawings, submitting applications, supervising the builder—according to your requirements. If you had a survey done of your house before buying it, the surveyor who did that job could be asked about the extension you now have in mind. To be sure of approaching the right kind of surveyor (there are surveyors who are not qualified in design and building work), you can write to the Royal Institution of Chartered Surveyors (29 Lincoln's Inn Fields, London WC2A 3DG) or to the Incorporated Association of Architects and Surveyors (24 Half Moon Street, London W 1Y 8BT) and ask for the names of building surveyors in your area.

Architects, building surveyors and consultants offer a range of services—from the first discussion and designs, to the preparation of the necessary documents and drawings getting approval from the various authorities, obtaining quotations and arranging contracts with builders, supervising work (to a greater or less degree) and authorising payments. You can make use of all these services, or seek professional advice at selected stages only.

But some are not interested in doing extensions to existing buildings, mainly because they are able to keep themselves occupied with larger—more lucrative—jobs. An architect who has recently set up on his own may be more willing to accept extension work; in an established firm, it may be given to a junior member. This can have the advantage that the architect involved may have plenty of time and interest to spend on your particular project.

In order to assess whether an architect, surveyor or consultant is likely to be satisfactory for your particular project, make an appointment to go to his office to discuss in general the extension scheme you have in mind. Some charge a small fee for a discussion of this sort.

You could ask to see drawings which have recently been prepared for a similar project. Ask also when he last submitted drawings for such a project to the relevant local authority and whether the drawings were approved at first submission.

If you approach an architect, an architectural consultant and a building surveyor in order to compare their proposals regarding your scheme, bear in mind that skilful design and technical competence are equally important for an extension.

An architect, a building surveyor or an architectural consultant should be able to give you a rough idea of the approximate cost of the scheme, including his fee for the part you want him to play.

fees

The fees charged by registered architects are determined by the extent of the services provided and are a percentage of the total cost (which cannot be known until the work is complete). The RIBA publishes a scale of minimum charges to which all its members must adhere: they must not charge less, and higher fees must be agreed beforehand between architect and client.

The minimum RIBA fee for what is called normal service for work on an existing building is 13 per cent for jobs costing up to £2,500, $12\frac{1}{2}$ per cent for jobs between £2,500 and £8,000, 12 per cent for jobs between £8,000 and £14,000.

Normal service an architect offers includes advising on alternative possibilities, preparing drawings from specific instructions, submitting the necessary information for approval to the local authority, drawing up specifications or other particulars required for obtaining tenders, preparing a contract, advising on the engagement of a builder and specialist consultants if required, preparing a timetable, supervising the work, issuing certificates for payment—and generally seeing the job right through. You may not need him to undertake all of this for your particular scheme.

If the architect is not required to provide the full normal service, the RIBA lays down a scale of fees to be charged for a partial service. Details of architects' fees and services are given in a booklet *Conditions of Engagement* issued by the RIBA (66 Portland Place, London W1N 4AD), price 40p.

An architect's fee for normal service is exclusive of the cost of prints and other reproductions of drawings and documents needed for submission to authorities, of travelling and other expenses. A separate, non-percentage, charge is made for these. Separate fees are charged for designs for fittings or furniture, garden layout or heating installations and similar extras.

Other services not included in the RIBA percentage fee are preparing any additional special drawings, handling any negotiations that may arise from an application for approval, obtaining any licences required (from a landlord or the freeholder, for example), valuing work when carried out. The architect should be able to tell you in advance what he will charge for any of these services. An architect is entitled to charge for amending working drawings following a client's later change of instruction, and to charge in respect of any work included in the original drawings but subsequently not carried out. He is also entitled to ask for payment of his fee in instalments at set stages of the work.

If you keep the cost of the extension down by providing some of the materials or carrying out some of the work yourself, you still have to pay the architect a fee based on what the work would have cost if the builder had carried it all out. So if the cost would have been £1,500 and you have reduced this to £1,200 by providing the bricks (from an old outhouse that you have knocked down, for instance), the architect will charge his percentage on the £1,500.

The basic charges of building surveyors are similar to those of architects—they use the RIBA scale. You should ask during your initial discussion how much the surveyor would charge for the work you want him to do. The Incorporated Association of Architects and Surveyors will give advice and information to a member of the public about the terms of employment and minimum charges for their building surveyor members.

Fees charged by individuals who are not members of one of the professional bodies are not controlled in any way. They are often considerably less than the RIBA scale fees for similar services. Find out what professional services a consultant offers and what fees he would charge for the particular services you think you are likely to need. An architectural consultant will wish to see the site before giving you a written quotation of the fee he will charge for his services.

The architect, surveyor or other consultant whom you engage should make it clear to you what is included in the charge he quotes and what he will charge for any other services or advice you ask him for later on.

The services of an architect or surveyor or other professional consultant are subject to value added tax (except where the services are provided by a builder or one of his employees).

Builders

If—in the case of a very simple extension perhaps—you decide not to have an architect or consultant, you should show your sketch plan to a builder and ask him to come and discuss the scheme and to give an estimate.

There is no general guide to choosing a good builder for a comparatively simple house extension. The names of local builders can be found in the telephone directory's yellow pages and advertisements in local publications. Builders generally put up their sign boards outside houses where they are working. Regional branches of the National Federation of Building Trades Employers and regional offices of the Federation of Master Builders can be asked for the names of local builders who might be suitable for extension projects. The engineer and surveyor's department of some local authorities keeps a list of builders in the area.

Generally, the best way to get a good builder is through a recommendation, either from someone you know well who has previously engaged the builder for similar work, or from an architect or consultant who knows local builders and the type of work to which they are best suited. The local authority building inspector is likely to have a good idea of the quality of work done by local builders. Before engaging again a builder you have yourself used for another job and found satisfactory, ensure that he is familiar with and capable of carrying out the type of scheme now envisaged. Ask whether the builder has recently carried out any similar scheme, and where you can see some of his workmanship; a good builder is only too pleased to show off his work.

Good builders are invariably popular so, if timing is important, it is wise to approach prospective firms well in advance of the time when you would like work to be started: six months' notice is not excessive.

Estimates should be obtained from two or three builders. Explain as exactly as possible the work to be carried out, making use of any sketches you have made. If any aspect of the scheme seems complicated, the builder may require more specific details. A builder, although prepared to give a free estimate for one scheme, will probably not welcome being asked to give successive estimates for a series of alternatives, so you should have a clear idea of what you want.

Any builder who is already engaged on an extensive programme of work may be unable or unwilling to commit himself to more. Or he may be unwilling to give an estimate if he thinks the job is too small to be worth his while.

A builder calculates the approximate cost at this stage by multiplying either the net floor area or the net cubic content of the new structure by a rate per square or cubic metre. The rate varies considerably, depending on the firm's overheads including wages, the type of work being undertaken, and local conditions and prices for materials.

The construction (including extension and improvement) of a building is zero-rated for value added tax, so a builder can claim back the VAT he has to pay on the materials he buys for use in such work. Therefore, he should not charge you for VAT on the materials he uses (unless for any reason he is not VAT-registered). You have to pay VAT on any materials you buy yourself. Value added tax is chargeable on work that counts as repair work and on items that are replacements.

package deal firms

Some firms of builders offer a package deal which includes taking measurements at the site, preparing drawings and other documents, making all necessary local authority applications, arranging finance, and carrying out the building work.

A package deal firm does not offer any more than can be obtained elsewhere from two or three different sources. The advantage is that you have to deal with only one firm for everything, and blame—if anything goes wrong—can therefore not be shifted. The main disadvantage is that you are putting all your eggs into one basket and have no professional adviser on your side.

A package deal firm quotes one price to cover everything involved in the job. Because this includes work normally carried out by an architect or other professional consultant and because the firm is taking a gamble by quoting a price before it has detailed drawings or specifications to go on, the quotation may be higher than one submitted by an ordinary builder for carrying out the construction work only.

If such a firm quotes a price lower than, or comparable with, quotations from at least two other builders (plus architectural fees) there should be no reason not to consider engaging the firm. Some firms require a deposit at the outset.

Since the builder is virtually drawing up his own instructions, it is important to ensure that he shows the scheme as you want it, not as he thinks it ought to be. You should read any form of contract very carefully, especially the small print, before committing yourself. For instance, some package deal firms' standard contract absolves the firm from responsibility for any alterations to the original plan, and consequent additional expense, that may become necessary once work has started. This condition would apply even if the alteration were due to a deficiency in the drawings which the firm itself had prepared, or to any miscalculation in design or specifications. If a contract appears too one-sided, you should insist that counter-conditions are incorporated in the agreement.

Finding the money

When you have obtained estimates from two or three builders, it is up to you to decide whether you can afford even the lowest. If you cannot, you must compromise with a smaller scheme. It is wise to allow a 10 per cent provision above any estimated cost to cover contingencies.

Before signing any contract, you should be sure that the money will be available, particularly if you plan to sell shares to get the necessary cash. If you intend to borrow part or all of the money, this is the moment to arrange the loan and check that you can afford the payments. Interest on a loan for improvements to your main home is one of the types of interest payments eligible for income tax relief. The *Money Which?* Tax-Saving Guide explains how this can effectively reduce the cost of borrowing; budget tax changes are reported on in the June issue of *Money Which?*

A mortgage can be arranged with a building society, an insurance company or a local authority. The maximum amount available and the maximum length of time over which repayments may be made vary with different sources. The deeds of the property will be held as security.

If you already have a mortgage, you may be able to get this increased for property improvement, particularly if you have paid off a substantial proportion of the original loan.

Insurance companies sometimes lend money on the security of the surrender value of an existing life insurance policy, or on the security of property.

You can try to get an ordinary or a personal loan from your bank. The maximum sum which can be obtained and the maximum length of time over which repayments may be made are determined by the bank manager, who will be influenced by your relationship with him, your ability to repay from income, securities which the bank may hold for you, the policy of his head office, and by current governmental lending restrictions.

A personal loan can also be obtained from a finance company specialising in short term loans for specific purposes. The maximum length of time over which repayments may be made is commonly 10 years. Some finance companies are prepared to grant credit facilities to house owners provided that the amount advanced does not exceed the current market value of the property or the difference between the market value and the amount still owed to a building society or local authority. A second mortgage can be obtained either direct from a finance company, or through a mortgage broker for a fee.

It is common for a lending organisation to require a surveyor's valuation of the property on which it is being asked to lend money. You have to pay the fee for the surveyor's report even if the organisation decides not to lend you any money.

Some local authorities make loans. The maximum amount which can be obtained and the maximum length of time over which repayments can be made are determined by individual local authorities whose decisions are dictated by their available funds. Local authorities usually lend money only for properties within their own area. You can get details from the treasurer's department of the local authority.

grants for house improvement
Local authorities administer and give grants (towards which the government contributes the greater part) for improving or renovating property. The amount of a grant is based on the eligible expense of the improvement or repair work; a maximum grant is 75 per cent if in a housing action area (90 per cent in cases of hardship); 60 per cent if in a general improvement area; 50 per cent elsewhere. The local council can tell you whether your house is in a housing action area or a general improvement area.

One grant, called an intermediate grant, is for providing for the first time certain basic standard amenities: basin, sink, hot and cold water supply, bath or shower, flush lavatory, coupled with essential repairs or replacements. You have a right to this grant if certain requirements are met: for example, that the building will comply with the Building Regulations as regards roof insulation.

The eligible expense limit is £700, made up of maximum amounts for each amenity, plus £800 for repair or replacement work.

Unlike an intermediate grant to which one has a right, a grant for improvement of a property is paid at the local authority's discretion, and only for property with an existing rateable value below a specified limit (at present, £300 in Greater London, £175 elsewhere). Improvement grants are to help owner-occupiers improve older houses to a good standard—they are not intended to assist with improvements to modern houses or fully equipped houses in good repair, nor normally for adding more bedroom space. An extension which simply gives you (or your car) more room to live in will probably not qualify. The local authority has to be satisfied that the property will meet certain standard requirements when the work has been done.

The maximum eligible expense for a house is £3,200, and the grant will be 50 per cent (or 75 per cent or 60 per cent in certain areas of the country). The local authority may be prepared to give a loan to applicants who have difficulty in providing their own part of the cost of the work.

Anyone who is a freeholder, or a leaseholder with at least five years unexpired on the lease, may apply for either type of grant. You have to declare that you intend to keep the house for some years—if you sell within, say, five years, you may have to repay part of the grant. No grant is given for the improvement of property used by an owner-occupier as a second home.

The work must not be started until the grant application has been approved, otherwise the grant will not be given. The grant is normally not paid until the work has been completed and is to the satisfaction of the local authority; in some cases, a grant may be paid in instalments.

A booklet called *Your guide to house renovation grants* is available free from local authority offices, and many local authorities produce their own notes of guidance for prospective applicants. A report on grants for improving your home was published in *Which?* July 1976.

Planning permission

You may have to adapt your ideas in order to obtain planning permission. The Town and Country Planning Act 1971 states that planning permission is required for the carrying out of any development of land. The act defines development as "the carrying out of building, engineering, mining or other operations in, on, over or under land, or the making of any material change in the use of any buildings or other land". The act goes on to list certain operations which do not constitute development, such as work which affects only the existing interior of a building or which does not materially affect the external appearance of a building.

Some development (referred to as permitted development) can be undertaken without the permission of the local planning authority. This includes the enlargement of a dwelling house that does not exceed the cubic content of the original house by more than 50 cubic metres or one-tenth, whichever is the greater, subject to a maximum of 115 cubic metres. But the height of the enlarged building must not exceed the height of the original house, and no part project beyond the forwardmost part of the original house which faces a road.

The permitted development limit relates to the size of the original building, 'original' meaning the house as it was on 1 July 1948, or as it was built if after that date.

To assess the cubic capacity of a house, the floor area is calculated by measuring the sides externally, multiplying the length by the breadth, and multiplying that figure by the height of the house. This is quite straightforward if the house is a neat rectangle and the roof is flat, but it becomes more complicated if the house has odd angles and an uneven pitched roof. Most people need a professional to make the calculations.

Irrespective of the size and shape of the proposed extension, if it is to be at a bend of a road or near a junction or intersection and is likely to obstruct the view of anyone driving along the road, planning permission should be sought. And it may be necessary to get planning permission if you are making a new or enlarged means of access to a road, as may be the case when a new garage is being built.

The erection of a garage within the vicinity of a house is treated as the enlargement of the house, but the erection of a small building such as a summerhouse or outhouse for the keeping of poultry, bees, pet animals, or livestock for the domestic needs or personal enjoyment of the occupants of the house, is not. These types of outbuilding, and small porches, domestic oil storage tanks, and gates, walls and fences, all count as permitted development but with restrictions on their size. Also, a hard-standing for a private vehicle is permitted development, as is the painting of the outside of a building.

If you are thinking of building an extension as a self-contained flat (for elderly parents, for instance), you should check early on how your local authority might view such an application: it can be regarded as a change of use—from a single family dwelling to a house occupied by more than one family. Many local authorities do not look favourably on this kind of project because it creates two separate dwellings instead of one, thus increasing the density of housing in the area. They may make it a requirement that the extension is not wholly self-contained—without a separate kitchen, for example—and is connected to the main house in such a way that it cannot later be sold as a separate dwelling.

The local authority when considering an application for planning permission for an extension to the front or the side of a house pays particular attention to the external appearance of the proposed new part, in order to ensure that it will harmonise with the existing building and adjoining buildings. If the scheme is considered detrimental to the visual amenities of the area, or detrimental to the amenities of neighbouring properties, planning permission may be refused.

Because a two-storey extension is more noticeable than a single-storey one, the local planning authority may be more strict about its external appearance. To be acceptable to a local authority, the finished structure must look right: it should blend in with the building to which it is joined, and harmonise with the general character of the neighbourhood. This can make it difficult to get planning permission for an extension to a house in a housing estate where the houses are designed with a uniformity of appearance.

Planning is concerned with public rather than private rights. There is, for example, no right to a view, but a neighbour may raise objections if a new structure would unduly interfere with the daylight to, or the view from, any windows in his house, or if it contains windows through which the neighbour's property would be directly overlooked. The question of overlooking is one on which there are no general rules and each case is determined by the local planning authority.

All these points should be taken into account by an architect or building surveyor or consultant at the design stage. You should consider them at the outset and, if in any doubt, get advice from the planning office of your local authority.

The Department of the Environment and the Welsh Office publish a series of *Development Control Policy Notes* for people wishing to extend or alter their house, and also a free booklet *Planning permission: a guide for householders.*

listed buildings

If your property is included in the list of buildings of special architectural or historic interest, you need authorisation before altering or extending the building in any manner which would affect its character.

If you think your property may, by reason of its age or character, be included in the list, you should go to your local authority offices and ask to inspect the schedule of listed buildings.

Demolition of any part of a building that is within a designated conservation area requires authorisation. Each local authority keeps maps showing the conservation areas in its district, so you should check whether your house is in a conservation area before any walls or outbuildings are knocked down.

The Building Regulations

Anyone contemplating extending his home has to observe certain laws. A comprehensive list of all the acts and regulations which relate to building would name hundreds of documents. Relating to a house extension, the most important is the Building Regulations.

The Public Health Act 1936 empowered local authorities to make their own by-laws relating to buildings and sanitation. The result was that authorities throughout the country each had their own set of by-laws. The Building Regulations which first came into effect in February 1966 took the place of local building by-laws. (When builders refer to 'the by-laws' they really mean the Building Regulations.) Following several amendments, the Regulations were completely revised and metricated, as the Building Regulations 1972, and with subsequent amendments have been consolidated into the Building Regulations 1976.

The Building Regulations operate throughout England and Wales with the exception of inner London where the GLC's by-laws apply. 'Inner' London means the area which was under the control of the London County Council before the creation of the Greater London Council in April 1965. London boroughs which were not in the old LCC area are covered by the Building Regulations.

The Building Regulations is a document of over 300 pages. There are 16 general regulations dealing with the interpretation of the regulations and their application; 4 regulations dealing with the fitness of materials to be used: 10 regulations about the preparation of the site, dealing with the protection of ground floors, the protection of walls, the prevention of damp, weather resistance; 20 regulations dealing with structural stability; 19 regulations dealing with structural fire precautions; 4 regulations dealing with means of escape in case of fire; 4 regulations dealing with the thermal insulation of roofs, walls and floors; 6 regulations dealing with the sound insulation of walls and floors; 7 regulations dealing with stairways, ramps, balustrades and vehicle barriers; 4 regulations dealing with refuse disposal; 8 regulations dealing with the open space required outside windows of habitable rooms, the height of rooms and ventilation; 22 regulations dealing with general and structural requirements for chimneys, flues, hearths and fireplaces; 12 regulations dealing with heat-producing appliances; 17 regulations dealing with drainage, private sewers, and cesspools; 4 regulations dealing with water closets and sanitary accommodation.

There are also 12 schedules to the Building Regulations. They contain various technical specifications and the procedure for giving notice. In general, any person who intends to erect any building; or make any structural alteration or extension to a building; or execute any work or install any fittings in connection with a building; or make any material change in the use of a building, is required to give notice to the local authority and supply detailed specifications, including the proposed methods of construction and materials to be used.

The schedules also include the designation of partially exempted buildings. These include a single storey building which is used exclusively for recreation or storage purposes (such as a summerhouse, aviary, greenhouse, conservatory, coal shed, garden tool shed, or potting shed) or a garage, if such a building is wholly detached from any other building and has a floor area of not more than 30 square metres.

A copy of the Building Regulations can be bought from Her Majesty's Stationery Offices (the 1976 Regulations cost £3.30) or through booksellers, or can be consulted in local authority offices or in most public reference libraries. The regulations are complex and difficult for a qualified person to interpret, let alone a layman who would almost certainly need professional advice. A report on the legal aspects of do-it-yourself in the May 1977 *Handyman Which?* includes a discussion of guides to the Building Regulations.

The siting, design and construction of an extension has to conform to the relevant parts of the Building Regulations. The regulations are more exacting with regard to habitable rooms. A habitable room is a room used for living accommodation, such as a bedroom, living room, sitting room, dining room, study, but not a bathroom nor a hall. A scullery or kitchen (unless it is also capable of being used as a breakfast room or dining room) does not count as a habitable room except for ventilation requirements.

The Building Regulations must be taken into account when deciding how the extension should be designed and built. Details of the proposed construction and materials have to be submitted to the local authority before any work is started, to show that the work will conform to the Building Regulations. Your architect or other professional consultant, or the builder, will point out any modifications that have to be made to your original ideas. The local authority building control officer (often still referred to as the building inspector) can also be asked for advice.

Siting

Certain requirements depend on where you want to extend. At the back of the house, problems will arise if you want to build directly over existing drains or up against any part of a boundary between two properties. Drains are more commonly situated at the back of a house than the front, and proximity to a boundary could present difficulties because of the requirements for fire precautions.

If you want to build at the side of the house, similar problems are likely to arise if drains run along the side of the building, or the side boundary is close.

It is wise not to seal off the rear of a property completely when building an extension on to the side. You should leave at least 1 metre (about 3 feet 3 inches) between the side boundary and any building to ensure that there is permanent access from the front of the building to the rear, if only so that the dustbins can be emptied without having to be carried through the house.

An extension which would project beyond the forwardmost part of a house or neighbouring building may not be permitted. If the local authority's building line for the street is in line with the front of the existing building, you are not likely to get permission for an extension to the front of the house. The same restriction on building lines can occur at the side of a property flanking a side street, and may forbid a promising sideways extension.

If you are considering an extension, particularly a two-storey one, which will be on or within inches of a boundary with a neighbour's property, it is a good idea to mention the proposed extension to your neighbour in the first instance. Some local planning authorities ask for neighbours' comments when determining a planning application in these circumstances. If you have an awkward neighbour who is likely to object, it is better to find out before going to the expense of having drawings prepared.

If an external wall is going to be directly adjacent to the boundary of your property, the owner of the adjoining property must give permission if the foundations for the wall would encroach over the boundary, even though the wall itself will be entirely within your property. So when planning your scheme, you should ask your neighbour, where necessary, if he has any objection to the foundations being constructed under his land. If he agrees, he should do so formally in writing, with reference to a plan of the site, so that there would be no difficulty later if he should sell his property. If your neighbour does not agree, it will mean changing your plans so that neither the wall nor the foundations trespass.

It is possible that you may need extra land for your extension. If your neighbour is willing to sell, make an offer for the extra land subject to obtaining planning permission. A reasonable neighbour would offer you an option to purchase at an agreed price, and within a reasonable period, the option lapsing automatically (with no hard feelings) if planning permission is refused. If planning permission is delayed, you should try to negotiate an extension of the option period.

The state of the ground may affect the choice of site. Foundations for an extension should not be on ground which has been made up in any way from its natural level, because there is a risk of subsidence or settling of the ground later on. In such a case, the area would first have to be excavated down to the original ground level.

External walls

External walls of all buildings must comply with the regulations about fire precautions. This can have a considerable effect on the positioning and general design of an extension. The theory behind these regulations is that a fire shall be prevented from spreading from one building to another across a boundary between two properties. It is proximity to the boundary of your property that determines the fire resistance required and the amount of unprotected area permitted in a particular wall.

The fire precaution regulations are complicated. A builder will have some general knowledge on the subject, but is unlikely to be knowledgeable about the more complex points of detail. You will have to find out from the architect or surveyor or consultant the precise details about what restrictions apply to your particular circumstances. You should tell the architect or consultant what windows and doors and other openings you would like to have in the external wall and what material you would like the wall made of, but must be prepared for him to tell you that you will have to amend your ideas because of the fire regulations.

fire resistance

Fire resistance is expressed as the length of time for which a wall will resist fire. An external wall which is less than 1 metre from a boundary it faces must be half an hour fire resistant from both inside and outside, and must not have any combustible material fixed on to the outside surface. A boundary which is at right angles to a wall does not count, even if it is nearer to the wall than the facing one. If the wall of the building faces a street or a canal or a river, the boundary line is not the fence or wall or whatever marks the edge of the property but is an imaginary line along the centre of the street or canal or river.

If an external wall is 1 metre or more from the boundary, it needs to be fire resistant from the inside only; the outside can be covered with combustible material subject to the restrictions on unprotected areas.

Unprotected areas of an external wall are those areas which have no fire resistance—for example, windows, doors and any other openings in the wall, and any combustible cladding. (The outer covering of a wall is known as cladding.) Only a specified area of an external wall can be unprotected. This area can be calculated according to the length of the wall and its distance from the boundary the wall faces. This restricts the total area of windows and other openings you can have in the wall.

So if you want your extension to be covered externally with a combustible material, such as timber boards, and the building is fairly close to a boundary, you must be prepared to be restricted on the aggregate area of doors and windows. For instance, if the wall of an extension is going to be nearer than 1 metre to the boundary, you cannot have a full-size window or ordinary door in that wall. (Fire-resistant doors are obtainable, made of solid asbestos sheets faced with plywood. They are heavier and more expensive than ordinary doors.) If you want to have a lot of windows in the new wall you must build the extension at least 6 metres (20 feet) from the boundary it will face. There are no restrictions about unprotected areas in the external wall of an average house if the boundary is more than 6 metres away.

B

FIRE RESISTANCE

Unprotected areas in external walls depend
on the distance of a wall from the boundary
it faces.
For a house of not more than three storeys :

If the least distance between the external wall and the boundary which it faces is	and the length of that wall is not more than	the total unprotected area must not exceed	see illus- trations below
less than 1 metre		nil	A
1 m or more, but less than 2·5 m	24 m	5·6 square metres	B
1 m or more, but less than 6 m	24 m	15 square metres	C
5 m or more	12 m	NO LIMIT	D
6 m or more	24 m	NO LIMIT	E

*If these dimensions are exceeded, this table cannot be used,
and complicated calculations are necessary.*

PLAN   ELEVATION

(A)

EXTENSION   HOUSE   EXTENSION   HOUSE

BOUNDARY

LESS THAN 1 m

NO UNPROTECTED
AREAS PERMITTED

NOT MORE THAN 24 m

(B) NOT MORE THAN 24 m

EXTENSION   HOUSE   EXTENSION   HOUSE

BOUNDARY

1 m OR MORE

UP TO 5·6 SQ. m
OF UNPROTECTED
AREAS PERMITTED

PLAN ELEVATION

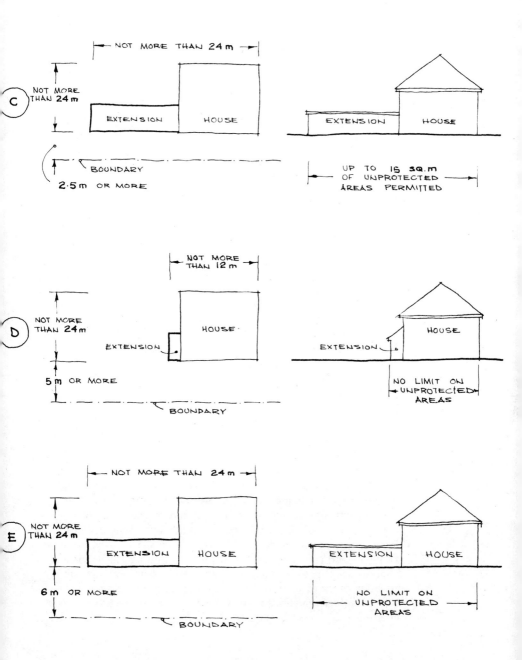

C

NOT MORE THAN 24 m

NOT MORE THAN 24 m

EXTENSION   HOUSE

BOUNDARY

2·5 m OR MORE

EXTENSION   HOUSE

UP TO 15 SQ.m OF UNPROTECTED AREAS PERMITTED

D

NOT MORE THAN 12 m

NOT MORE THAN 24 m

HOUSE

EXTENSION

5 m OR MORE

BOUNDARY

EXTENSION   HOUSE

NO LIMIT ON UNPROTECTED AREAS

E

NOT MORE THAN 24 m

NOT MORE THAN 24 m

EXTENSION   HOUSE

6 m OR MORE

BOUNDARY

EXTENSION   HOUSE

NO LIMIT ON UNPROTECTED AREAS

The maximum unprotected area permitted is the total permitted area in both the external wall of the extension and that of the house. In all cases, the critical distance on which the area depends is the distance between the boundary and the nearer of the two walls.

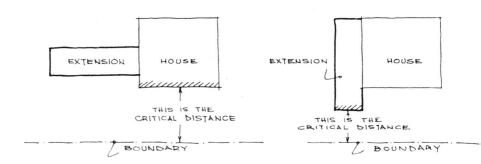

No account need be taken of an unprotected area which does not exceed 1 square metre if it is at least 4 metres from any other unprotected area in the same side of the building, nor of an unprotected area not exceeding one-tenth of a square metre (about 150 square inches) if this is at least 1·5 metres from another unprotected area. This means that you can have small windows or outlets such as air bricks in an external wall without counting them as unprotected areas. Glass bricks are also considered sufficiently fire resistant, so there is no restriction on how much of a wall is made of glass bricks.

insulation

Every substance transmits heat to a greater or a less degree, and it is possible to calculate the heat loss through any of the types of material used for an external wall. The Building Regulations specify what thermal insulation must be provided to reduce the loss of heat, and list various types of construction which are deemed to achieve this.

Walls can be of solid construction or cavity built. Nowadays external walls to habitable rooms are nearly always cavity walls, to comply not only with rules about thermal insulation but also those about protection against damp penetration. A cavity wall consists of two separate thin walls, called leaves or skins, built side by side with an air space between them. The two leaves are held together by small metal strips or loops of wire (known as wall ties), and form one integral wall. A wall of cavity construction must be made of leaves of specified materials and thickness to meet the requirements for thermal insulation. Most cavity walls are constructed with an outer leaf of bricks and an inner leaf of lightweight concrete blocks.

In a solid wall, the simplest way of providing sufficient thermal insulation is to construct it of cellular or aerated concrete blocks at least 200 mm (about 8 inches) thick and of a specific density. Bricks on their own do not provide sufficient thermal insulation for solid walls and are therefore rarely used for the external walls of habitable rooms.

For the sake of insulation, the total area of glazing in a new external wall is restricted to a percentage of the wall area; the percentage is greater with double glazing.

materials

A condition of being granted planning permission may be that the external appearance of an extension should match that of the existing house. This would present no problems if the house was itself built fairly recently. But if the house was built earlier in the century, or even longer ago, it could be that the bricks used for its external walls are no longer manufactured. Your only chance of getting any to match would be to try to buy the same or similar type of brick secondhand, perhaps from a building being demolished in the area.

There are many kinds of new brick, varying in price and type according to the part of the country. Bricks are suitable for external walls without any additional weathering surface. The alternative to bricks is concrete blocks. Concrete blocks are more expensive than bricks but cheaper to lay, and for an outside wall need cladding or have to be rendered—that means coating them with a cement surface.

Bricks and blocks made to metric standards differ in size from those made to traditional (imperial) measurements, so if you need to match existing walls, you may have to search for bricks or blocks of the appropriate size.

An architect, building surveyor or architectural consultant, and a builder, should be able to tell you about the various bricks and blocks that are available, with the range of prices and sizes, and advise about the most suitable to choose for your extension.

Internal walls

The construction of internal walls—that is, any walls that divide up the extension inside—do not have to conform to any regulations about fire precautions or thermal insulation. They just have to be strong enough to do the job for which they are intended.

Internal walls which support any part of the ceiling or roof should be constructed of bricks or blocks at least 75 mm (about 3 inches) thick. A non-loadbearing wall, being no more than a partition—and sometimes referred to, therefore, as a partition wall—can be of timber frame construction (also called studding).

Where the weight of a partition wall has to be kept to a minimum, as it would on an upper floor, for instance, a timber frame wall would be preferable, but in ground floor extensions where foundations can be provided to support the wall, a solid wall is the more usual choice.

A solid partition wall is likely to be slightly more expensive than an equivalent timber frame wall but is more substantial. It usually reduces sound transmission between rooms to a greater extent than a timber construction that is not specifically designed to be sound-resisting. Sound insulation may be important between say, a living room and an adjoining bedroom, or between a lavatory and a living room.

Floors

There are two principal types of floor construction for ground floor extensions; solid and suspended. In the solid form of construction, there is no air space between the foundation and the floor. In a solid floor, a damp-proof layer, called the damp-proof membrane, must be built in and joined to a damp-proof course in the external walls so that moisture or damp is not transmitted to the building.

In the suspended type of floor, there is an air space between the foundation and the floor itself. Damp is prevented from reaching the floor timber by the formation of a damp-proof course in the brickwork supporting the floor.

The decision whether to have a solid or a suspended floor in a ground floor extension may be influenced by the difference in levels of the existing building and the adjacent ground where the new part is to be built. For example, if the ground falls away sharply at the point where you want to build an extension, it would be expensive to have a solid floor constructed because of the depth of concrete that would be needed to build up the level.

Another factor affecting choice of floor construction is the type of top floor covering you plan to have. For wall-to-wall carpeting, for instance, which has to be fixed at the edges to timber boards, a suspended floor with timber boards would probably be the better choice, as a solid floor would need to have some means of anchorage added, such as timber battens. On the other hand, a covering of plastic tiles or sheeting, or of cork tiles, can be laid straight on top of a solid floor but a suspended floor construction would need an additional layer of hardboard between the timber boards and the covering.

Upper floor extension

If you want to build over the top of an existing single-storey structure, you should first find out whether the additional weight will harm any part of the existing structure. Foundations which were designed and built to support only a single storey might not be capable of safely supporting additional loads: for example, the foundations for a garage would be inadequate.

It is unlikely that you will be able to tell whether the existing foundations are adequate without taking professional advice. An architect or consultant will probably charge for advising on the problem. Some excavation may be necessary. If you are able to get your local building control officer to make an inspection, he will give his advice free. Building control officers are under no obligation to carry out an inspection of this sort, but most will do so. If your house is of post-war construction, he may be able to check from the plans kept in his office.

If the existing foundations are not capable of supporting any additional weight, an upper floor can be constructed only if the foundations are improved or renewed. The alternative, and probably the best, course of action is to demolish existing walls that will have to bear additional weight and then construct new foundations for them. The cubic content of any structure that has to be demolished and reconstructed does not have to be counted in the cubic content calculations to check whether planning permission is required for an extension (that is, where it is more than 50 cubic metres).

If the existing ground floor structure does not have cavity walls or thick enough solid walls (a garage might well fall into this category), there will not be adequate support for the cavity walls needed for a habitable room at first floor level. If both the existing foundations and walls are adequate, the new external walls can safely be built up.

The joists in the structure of the existing roof are unlikely to be sufficient to carry the load of a floor, so new joists will have to be introduced to support the new floor.

The design and layout of a new staircase to an upper floor has to comply with the Building Regulations' requirements regarding headroom, steepness, width and general safety.

Planning permission may be conditional on the external appearance of the new structure blending in with that of the existing building. If the rest of the house has a pitched roof, joining a new pitched roof to an existing one can be tricky and expensive.

If a two-storey extension to the side of the building would completely seal off the rear access, it might be possible to build an extension solely at first floor level at the side of the house without any walls underneath—the support being provided by means of columns, or piers. The thickness of the piers will depend on the material of which they are made and their height—steel columns, for instance, can be slimmer than brick or timber ones but may not be visually acceptable. The underside, or 'ceiling', must be thermally insulated and have a layer of some moisture-resistant material. The space at ground floor level can be used for access from the front to the rear of the property or as a car port. As far as planning permission is concerned, the cubic content of such an extension is deemed to be not only the solid part at first floor level, but also the open part at ground floor level.

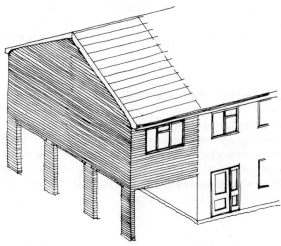

Roof

When deciding about the roof, you have to bear in mind that the ceiling of a habitable room must be at least 2·3 metres (about 7 feet 7 inches) above the finished floor level. The headroom in a bay window must be at least 2 metres.

flat roof

A flat roof consists of a waterproof covering over a deck which is supported by timber beams known as the roof joists. These joists also serve to hold the ceiling underneath. A flat roof is not dead level: it has to slope slightly so that rainwater runs off instead of ponding.

Standards of resistance to fire for all roofs are laid down according to the distance of the roof from the nearest boundary. There are various types of solid roof construction and covering which comply with these requirements in any situation: for instance, a deck made of timber board or wood-wool slabs, covered with metal sheets or with mastic asphalt or bitumen felt. A common type of deck is timber boarding 25 mm (about an inch) thick with a covering of two or three layers of asbestos-based bitumen felt.

The roof over living accommodation must have a prescribed degree of thermal insulation.

A flat roof is usually cheaper than the alternative, a sloping or pitched roof.

pitched roof

A pitched roof can be one of three kinds: gable-ended, hipped, lean-to.

You will probably want to match the tiles or slates on the new roof with those on the existing roof. The local planning authority may make stipulations about this. You can ask your architect or consultant about the various types of roof covering available. He should be able to show you some samples of tiles and slates, as well as manufacturers' brochures.

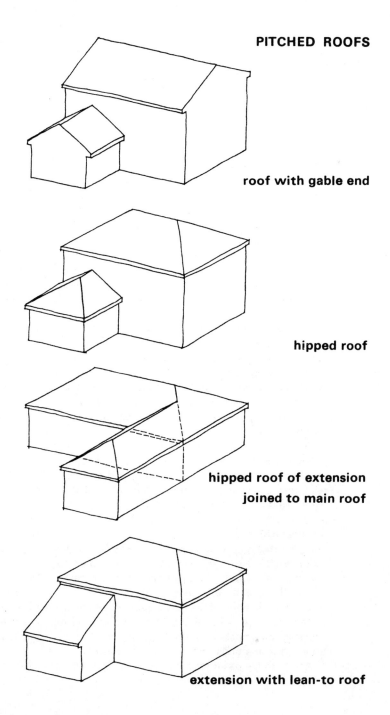

PITCHED ROOFS

roof with gable end

hipped roof

hipped roof of extension
joined to main roof

extension with lean-to roof

The type of slates or tiles to be used is affected by the slope of the roof, and this in turn may be dictated by the height to which the ridge can extend upwards. The shallower the slope of the roof, the longer the slates or tiles must be in order to obtain a large enough overlap to prevent rainwater from penetrating.

The more conventional types of roof covering, such as natural slates or asbestos-cement slates or clay or concrete tiles, present no fire hazard. But thatched roofs and coverings of wooden shingles or other combustible material do not meet the fire precaution regulations unless the building is a specified distance away from a boundary.

The prescribed degree of thermal insulation in a roof over living accommodation can be achieved in various ways, such as by placing glass fibre matting or quilting between the ceiling joists.

A translucent roof—invariably of lean-to construction—cannot be used on an extension for living accommodation because the required degree of thermal insulation cannot be achieved by any type of translucent roofing material. It can be used on a conservatory type of extension, a garage or store-room. Condensation is likely to occur under a translucent roof in cold weather.

Fire precaution regulations applying to translucent roofs vary according to the circumstances. They can be met by using wire reinforced pvc sheeting, certain grades of glass fibre sheeting, or wired glass.

Rainwater disposal

On a flat roof, guttering must be provided at the low side of the roof to which rainwater will flow because of the slope of the roof. One way of doing this is by carrying the roof deck and covering across the top of the external wall. The roof covering is then turned down over the edge of the deck in front of a vertical board known as the fascia, to which a conventional rainwater gutter is fixed. Similarly, on a pitched roof the gutter is fixed to the fascia board attached to the ends of the projecting rafters.

Another type of gutter construction is to build up the external wall as a parapet with a gutter concealed behind it, and either an external or an internal downpipe.

Which method of guttering you choose depends mainly on how you want the outside of the building to look. An internal rainwater pipe is the neatest but the most expensive and, if a blockage occurs inside the pipe, it is difficult to clear.

Rainwater gutters and downpipes are referred to as rainwater goods in the building trade. Every rainwater downpipe must be connected to a suitable outlet: it must not discharge on to the ground. In some cases, it is possible for a new rainwater pipe to discharge into an existing gutter, or to connect into an existing rainwater pipe, perhaps with the addition of a new hopper (an open funnel-shaped or rectangular fitting). But in most cases a complete new downpipe has to be provided.

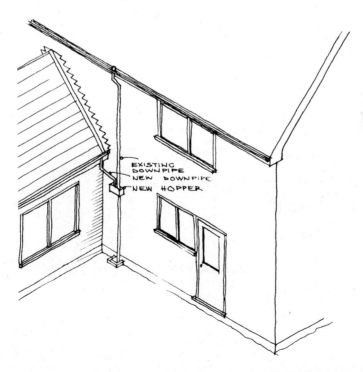

If there is an existing drain for rainwater (called a surface water drain) close by, the foot of the new downpipe can be connected to it, either direct to the drain underground or by discharging over a gully connected to it.

Where there is no surface water drain to connect to, a new one can be laid, connecting either to a public surface water sewer or to a soakaway. A soakaway is a pit in the ground filled with rubble or similar material which allows surface water to soak away into the surrounding subsoil. In districts with soil liable to become water-logged in winter or of low permeability—clay or hard chalk, for

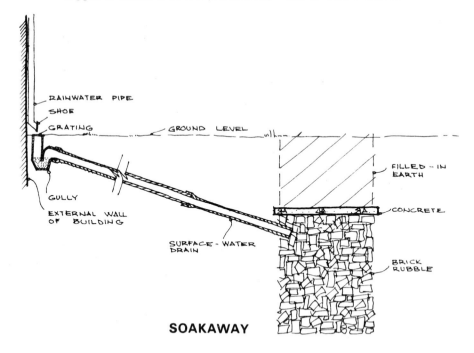

SOAKAWAY

instance—it may be necessary to provide a hollow soakaway which can take a greater quantity of rainwater. The water then gradually disperses into the surrounding soil through perforations in the soakaway's structure.

The soakaway has to be well away from any building, at a distance approved by the local authority. The top is filled in again with earth and can then be covered by a lawn, a flower bed, or anything else. For this reason it is generally difficult to know where an existing soakaway is. If you can find one and it is large enough, new rainwater pipes can be connected to it.

In cases where no surface water drains are available, the local authority may permit new rainwater pipes to be connected to existing soil drains. But there is a restriction on combining drains in this way because sewage works can overflow as a result of heavy rainstorms flooding the drains.

Alternatively, a large water butt can be placed so that the new downpipe discharges into it. Keen gardeners favour this method because the butt acts as a reservoir for watering their plants. But water butts can easily overflow, thus defeating their main purpose, and some local authorities insist on a butt being provided with an overflow connected to either a surface water drain or a soakaway.

Doors, windows and openings

Where a new opening is being made in a wall for a door or window, the wall over the opening must be strong enough to support the weight above it. This can be done by putting a small beam, called a lintol, across the top of the opening. It is cheaper if a new opening in an existing wall can be designed so that an existing beam can be left in place to support the remaining wall above; it is important that the existing beam has a sufficient amount of wall to rest on each side of the new opening.

When planning where to have the doors and windows in the extension, you also have to bear in mind the regulations about the lighting and ventilation of rooms and the structural stability of walls which contain door and window openings.

open space outside windows

There must be unobstructed space for at least 3·6 metres (about 12 feet) outside the window of a habitable room, open to the sky without any obstruction. In this context, your local authority may count a kitchen as a habitable room if it is also to be used, or is big enough to be used, for eating in as well as cooking. If a room has more than one window, the zone of open space can be shared between the windows or be outside only one of them.

The prescribed zone of open space is an imaginary shaft, rising from outside the lower level of the window up to the sky. The base of this imaginary shaft slopes at an angle of 30 degrees upwards from either the line of the lower window level (that is, the bottom of the glass in the window) or a line 1·2 metres (about 4 feet) above the level of the floor, whichever is the higher. The width of the shaft at the wall containing the window is calculated in proportion to the floor area of the room taking into account the window height. The outer side of the shaft—the side farthest away from the window—is parallel to the window and at least 3·6 metres away from it, and is at least 3·6 metres wide.

A zone of open space must be unobstructed by any rising

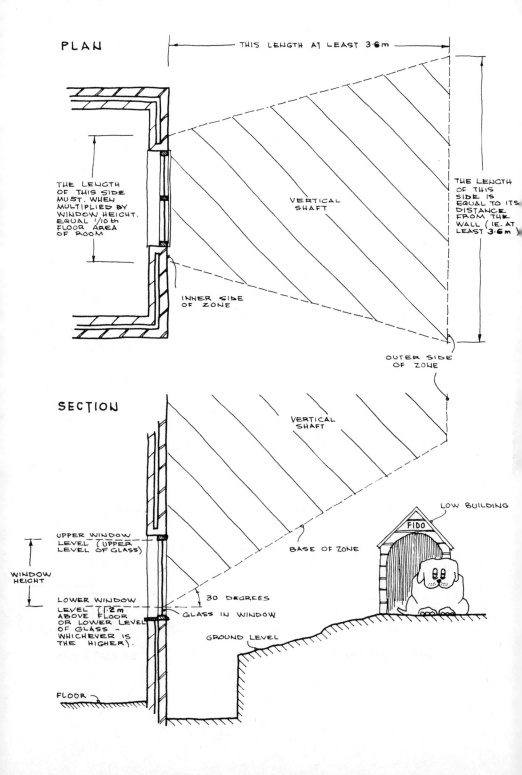

PLAN

THIS LENGTH AT LEAST 3·6m

THE LENGTH OF THIS SIDE MUST, WHEN MULTIPLIED BY WINDOW HEIGHT, EQUAL 1/10th FLOOR AREA OF ROOM

VERTICAL SHAFT

THE LENGTH OF THIS SIDE IS EQUAL TO ITS DISTANCE FROM THE WALL (IE. AT LEAST 3·6m)

INNER SIDE OF ZONE

OUTER SIDE OF ZONE

SECTION

VERTICAL SHAFT

LOW BUILDING

FIDO

UPPER WINDOW LEVEL (UPPER LEVEL OF GLASS)

BASE OF ZONE

WINDOW HEIGHT

30 DEGREES

LOWER WINDOW LEVEL (1·2m ABOVE FLOOR OR LOWER LEVEL OF GLASS - WHICHEVER IS THE HIGHER).

GLASS IN WINDOW

GROUND LEVEL

FLOOR

ground, a building or other structure outside the window (trees or bushes do not count). However, since the base of the zone slopes upwards, it is possible for a low building or a wall to be underneath the upward slope of the zone.

At least some part of the outer side of the shaft must be directly opposite some part of the window: the inner side of the imaginary shaft does not have to fall symmetrically over the width of the window. It is often possible, therefore, for the prescribed zone of open space to be achieved outside a window even where most of the window looks out on to a blank wall or other such obstruction.

The zone of open space outside any window should fall entirely over land belonging exclusively to the building containing the window, but if the property is bounded by a street or a canal or a river, the zone can extend halfway across the roadway or the water. On housing estates where there are no fixed boundaries,

plan view of overlapping zones of open space

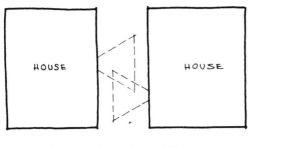

NOT   PERMITTED   PERMITTED

plan view of asymmetrical zone of open space

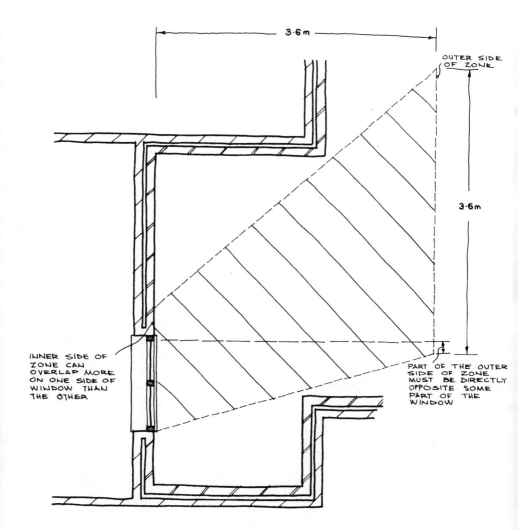

zones of open space outside windows are allowed to fall over communal land provided that no zone overlaps the zone for a window in another building. It is, however, permissible for zones to windows in the same building to overlap.

Some variations are permitted in the calculations for an open zone, so it is worth discussing any peculiar problems with the local authority building control officer.

No extension should be sited so that the zone of open space for an existing window is diminished. The exception, which applies to houses built before 1966, is that an extension consisting of a kitchen, a scullery or other outhouse, a bathroom or a lavatory, is allowed to reduce an existing habitable room's zone provided that there is an open space of at least 9 square metres (about 100 square feet) somewhere adjacent to the extension over land belonging exclusively to the house. This open space does not have to be directly outside the windows in question.

An existing window serving a habitable room can be blocked or enclosed provided another window to the room has the prescribed zone of open space outside it.

A conservatory or veranda or similar structure with a translucent roof can be added in front of an existing window even if it is the only window to the room; any extension with a solid roof must not project more than 1·5 metres (about 5 feet) in front of the wall containing the window. If the wall containing the window is removed and the whole room extended, there is no problem—provided there is the prescribed zone of open space outside the new window serving the enlarged room.

existing situation

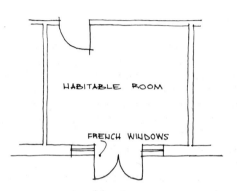

HABITABLE ROOM

FRENCH WINDOWS

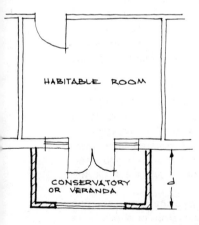

HABITABLE ROOM

CONSERVATORY
OR VERANDA

d

ROOF MUST BE
TRANSLUCENT
IF d IS MORE
THAN 1·5 m

permitted

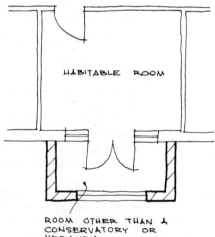

HABITABLE ROOM

ROOM OTHER THAN A
CONSERVATORY OR
VERANDA

not permitted

ventilation

Every new habitable room must be ventilated, either by mechanical means or by one or more ventilation openings whose total area is equal to at least one-twentieth of the floor area of that room. A window that can be opened, any hinged panel, adjustable louvre or other similar means of ventilation to the external air counts as a ventilation opening. Some part of the ventilation opening must be at least 1·75 metres (about 5 feet 9 inches) above the floor of the room. In practice, windows are the usual means of ventilation.

You must not add an extension which interferes with the required ventilation to an existing room. If the extension involves altering a window to an existing room, by bricking it up or turning it into a door to provide access to the extension, for example, the ventilation to the existing room must still meet the requirements. If you are building an extension leading off a room in an older house which does not have the degree of ventilation nowadays required, the existing room does not have to be made to comply with present ventilation requirements.

A door opening direct to the external air—for example, a french window—is not allowed to be the only ventilation opening to a room, even if, when open, the opening is larger than one-twentieth of the floor area. But if there is another ventilation opening of at least 10 000 square millimetres (about 15 square inches), perhaps a fanlight or a hinged flap, the door or french window can then count towards the total ventilation requirement for the room.

A habitable room, a kitchen or a scullery, can have its ventilation opening into an enclosed veranda, conservatory or similar area outside the room provided that the enclosed place has a means of ventilation to the external air with a total opening area equal to at least one-twentieth of the combined floor areas of the inside room plus the veranda or other outside area.

A room used for the storage of perishable food must be ventilated direct to the external air. The area providing ventilation does

VENTILATION AND OPEN SPACE TO WINDOWS OF EXISTING ROOM WHEN ADDING AN EXTENSION

THIS IS NOW THE ONLY WINDOW AND HAS TO PROVIDE THE RIGHT AMOUNT OF VENTILATION AND ZONE OF OPEN SPACE FOR THE WHOLE ROOM

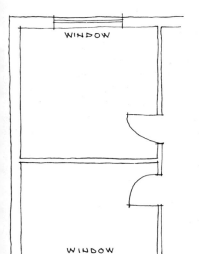

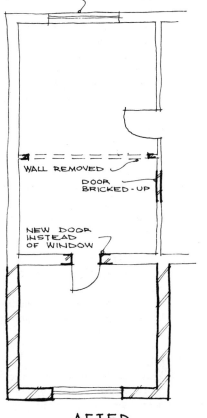

WALL REMOVED

DOOR BRICKED-UP

NEW DOOR INSTEAD OF WINDOW

WINDOW

WINDOW

BEFORE

AFTER

not have to be as large as for other rooms, but any opening has to have a fly-proof screen.

Ventilation to a room containing a lavatory must be direct to the external air and cannot be through any other room or enclosure. If the extension blocks an existing ventilating window to a kitchen or lavatory, alternative—mechanical—ventilation must be provided.

Wherever possible, you should avoid having to have the sole means of ventilation to a room provided mechanically by an extractor fan, but sometimes this is unavoidable. Mechanical ventilation is considered by most local authorities to be adequate provided the fan discharges direct to the external air and effects at least three changes of air per hour. Extractor fans are marked with their rate of extraction, and you have to calculate the size of fan needed according to the cubic content of the room to be ventilated.

Where mechanical ventilation is necessary because there is no window, the local authority usually require the extractor fan to be wired up to the light switch so that the fan operates automatically when the light is switched on; usually, a timing device is incorporated so that the fan continues to operate for some minutes after the light has been turned off.

Bathroom extension

A bathroom being installed in a house which did not have one before is eligible for a grant from the local authority.

The best position in which to put a bathroom depends on the layout of existing rooms and also on the location of the drains outside the house.

drainage

Drainage can be the most expensive part of any extension scheme. You should therefore try to plan your extension in such a way that it involves as little drainage work as possible, and you should stress to your architect, surveyor or consultant that drainage is to be kept to a minimum. Every length of underground drain adds to the cost, and each inspection chamber takes a substantial sum.

A drain is a pipe below ground level; pipes above ground level are not termed drains. Wash basins, baths, sinks, showers and bidets are known as waste appliances and all pipes above ground level conveying only water from such appliances are waste pipes. Lavatories are known as soil appliances and pipes above ground

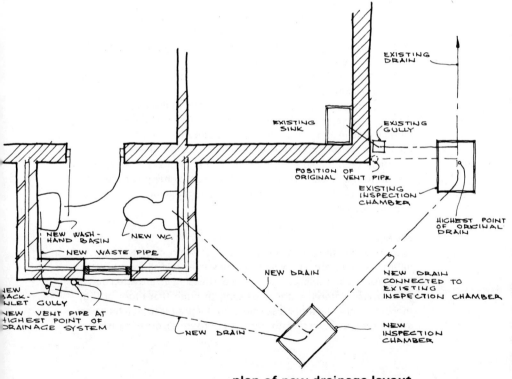

plan of new drainage layout

level conveying water from a soil appliance, either alone or together with waste water, are soil pipes. A pipe above ground level
which is open to the external air at its highest point and is
connected to the drainage system is a ventilation pipe.

A new connection to an existing drain is best made at an
existing inspection chamber. If there is not a conveniently situated
inspection chamber, a new one should be made. Every length of
drain must be laid in a straight line. Bends are only permitted if
there is an inspection chamber at every change of direction. Drains
are always laid starting from the lower end of the length of drain,
with the pipes sloping upwards towards the appliance or appliances to be drained. If existing drains are already near the surface,
it may not be possible to make a new connection to them with
sufficient slope. In such a case, a new set of drains will have to be
laid to the public sewer.

Every drainage system must be ventilated to the external air so
that any gases in the drains can escape. This is done through a
vertical pipe leading from the highest point of the drains. The pipe
runs from below ground level to above the top of any window,
generally terminating at roof level. If new drains are being connected to the existing drainage system at a higher point than the
existing ventilation pipe, the pipe will have to be moved, or a new
one introduced.

access
A room containing a lavatory must not open directly into any
habitable room, kitchen or scullery. However, it is allowed to open
into a room used solely for sleeping or dressing in, provided that it
can be also entered without passing through that room or that
there is another lavatory elsewhere on the premises which can be
entered without passing through a bedroom or dressing room.

If you want to add a bathroom extension to be approached from a kitchen or habitable room, the bathroom must not contain a lavatory. If it does, you will have to form a lobby between the new bathroom and the existing room. The local authority may insist that such a lobby must be ventilated direct to the external air. If space is very restricted, as is often the case at the rear of an older type of terraced house, it may not be possible to incorporate a lobby in this way. You can then overcome the problem by forming a separate space to contain the lavatory so that the remainder of the bathroom is the lobby. A space so formed to contain the lavatory must be a proper room with a door.

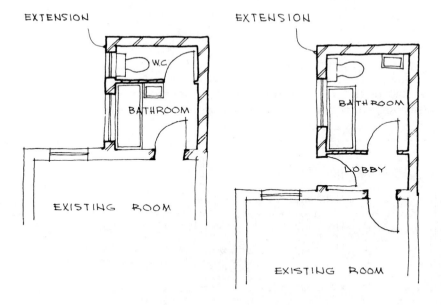

EXTENSION

W.C

BATHROOM

EXISTING ROOM

EXTENSION

BATHROOM

LOBBY

EXISTING ROOM

CONVERTING A BEDROOM INTO A BATHROOM

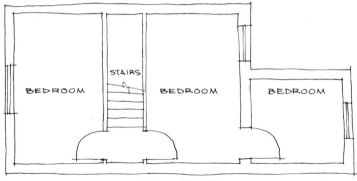

existing situation

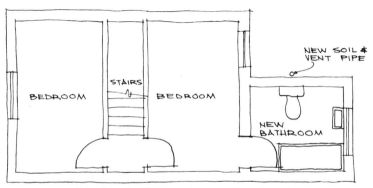

permitted only if there is another lavatory elsewhere in the house not opening into a bedroom

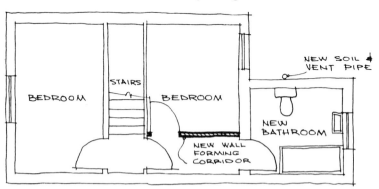

acceptable layout where the new bathroom contains the only lavatory in the house

It is sometimes possible to convert an existing bedroom into a bathroom. Many older houses were built to a design which has one bedroom leading off another, and the far room makes a good situation for a bathroom, especially if it is at the back of the house where the drains are. Because of the restrictions about a lavatory approached through a bedroom, it may be necessary to make a passage to the bathroom along one side of the bedroom.

plumbing

The Building Regulations are concerned only with the outlets of soil and waste appliances, not with hot and cold water supplies. But all plumbing must conform to the local water board's or water authority's requirements. Each has its own by-laws or regulations and the plumber who will make the connections to the existing pipes should be familiar with local requirements. He makes arrangements for inspection by the local water authority when required.

Some water boards allow direct supplies from the mains only to the cold water tap at the kitchen sink and to the storage cistern. All other cold water—supplied to bath, basins, shower, lavatory and water heaters—usually comes from the cold water storage cistern. The cistern has to be situated at a high enough level to ensure sufficient pressure at the outlets. The higher the level, the better the pressure, so a storage cistern is generally placed as high as possible, in the roof space of the house. If the cold water storage cistern cannot be high enough to feed a hot water cylinder with an electric immersion heater, it may be possible to install a combination unit which includes a small integral cold water cistern on top of the cylinder with the immersion heater. The unit must be placed above the level of the highest tap to be served. These units are also useful where space is restricted. They are made in round, oval and rectangular forms to fit into as small a space as possible.

If an instantaneous gas water heater is to be installed and it is impossible to provide sufficient pressure from the cold water cistern because of lack of available height in the building, the water for the heater has to come direct from the mains. The temperature of the hot water from an instantaneous gas heater varies according to the rate of flow into the heater, and if this fluctuates, which is likely to happen in the mains supply unless a water pressure governor has been fitted, the water may not be hot enough on some occasions.

Heating installations

The Building Regulations are not concerned with heating appliances run off electricity, but they control the installation of any other heating or cooking appliance.

You should ensure that the extension you are now putting up is designed in such a way that it will not prejudice a heating installation you may want later. If you discuss your ideas for any future installation with your architect or consultant, he can suggest appropriate action now. If, for example, you are thinking of having solid fuel central heating for the house at some time, and you are building on a kitchen or utility room extension, now is the time to have a chimney built or provision made for a flue, to avoid extra expense and inconvenience later.

A flue is the void through which smoke, fumes and gaseous discharges pass, not the pipe or structure forming the void. The pipe is referred to as a flue pipe and a chimney is that part of the structure of a building which forms a flue. For example, the space within a brick-built chimney is the flue. Most heat-producing appliances must be connected to a flue, in the form of either a chimney or a flue pipe. Unflued appliances can lead to condensation trouble, but some oil-burning and gas appliances are designed to operate without being connected to any kind of flue.

If a new chimney has to be constructed on an extension, it should go on one of the new walls rather than on the existing wall from which the extension is being built, because to put a chimney up against an existing wall would involve rebuilding that wall.

A new chimney can be built with insulated metal pipes; if of masonry, it must be either lined or constructed of a special type of concrete block to prevent the discharged gases from attacking the surrounding structure. (A chimney for just one gas fire or heater can be made of brick without being lined.) But a new appliance (or fireplace) can be connected to an existing chimney that is not lined if the chimney was built before the introduction of the Building Regulations. For a gas-burning or oil-burning appliance, however, it is advisable to have an existing chimney lined. This overcomes problems which could arise from defects within the structure of the chimney, such as condensation or leaking fumes.

The Consumer Publication *Central heating* includes detailed information on the choice of systems, fuels and appliances.

solid fuel and oil

If you decide to have an open fire, burning a solid fuel, it must be installed on what is referred to as a constructional hearth. This type of hearth must be incorporated into the floor at the time the floor is being constructed, so it should be included at the design stage. The hearth must be of non-combustible material and must be a minimum thickness and a minimum distance from the wall, as specified in the Building Regulations.

For an open fire, there are various regulations about the construction and thickness of the fireplace structure and about the ventilation of the room, and restrictions on the proximity of combustible materials in and around the fireplace.

A solid fuel or oil-fired boiler has to have a constructional hearth built as an integral part of the floor. If the boiler is being put in a fireplace recess which conforms to the relevant regulations about such factors as thickness and non-combustible materials, it can be positioned flush against the back wall of the recess. Otherwise, the boiler must be put a specified distance away from the wall. In the case of any type of boiler, there are regulations to ensure that the flue is accessible for cleaning and for clearing out the condensation that accumulates within the flue.

Requirements for the ventilation of a room where a solid fuel or oil-burning boiler is installed depend on the type of heating installation.

A flue pipe from a solid fuel or oil-burning appliance has either to pass through an external wall of the room, or to discharge into a chimney.

The outlet of the flue pipe or chimney must be a specified height above the roof from which it emerges and above windows, skylight or ventilators, and above the top of any nearby building —generally, this height is 1 metre (about 3 feet 3 inches); near the ridge of a pitched roof it may only have to be 600 mm (about 2 feet). The height is exclusive of the height of any chimney pot or other flue terminal.

gas appliances

Most gas appliances must be separated from any combustible material in the structure of the building either by a shield of noncombustible material or by an air space.

The size of a room containing a gas appliance and the type of appliance affect the amount of ventilation that has to be provided in the form of windows, airbricks or louvres. The local gas region can be consulted about the ventilation needed in your proposed scheme.

Most floor-mounted gas appliances must be installed on an area of non-combustible material at least 12·5 mm (about half an inch) thick and of the dimensions specified in the Building Regulations. It is easier to construct this hearth area when the floor is being put down, although one can be formed later without too much disturbance.

The flue requirements of a space heater depend on the size of the room.

Some gas appliances do not connect directly to a flue: a gas cooker does not, nor a water heater below a certain thermal rating—for instance, a sink water heater. You can install a gas water heating appliance without connecting it to a flue only if the room is large enough and has a specified amount of permanent ventilation and a ventilation opening. In a bathroom, a gas water heater should be of the room-sealed type with a balanced flue.

Where a flue pipe from a gas appliance passes through an internal wall, floor or the roof, there are certain restrictions. Nowhere is any part of the flue pipe allowed to be nearer than 50 mm (about 2 inches) to any combustible material.

The top outlet of a flue from a gas appliance must have a terminal fitting which lets the gaseous discharges out freely but minimises down-draught and prevents anything from getting into the flue that might obstruct it. It must not be placed nearer than 600 mm (about 2 feet) to any window, skylight or similar air inlet.

If you have a gas appliance with a balanced flue installed, you do not have to worry about a chimney or special flue pipe through the building and, because no combustion air is taken from within the room, there is no need to provide permanent ventilation to the room. Balanced flue boilers are relatively small and can be wall-mounted to release floor space for other purposes.

outlets of flues from solid fuel or oil-burning appliances

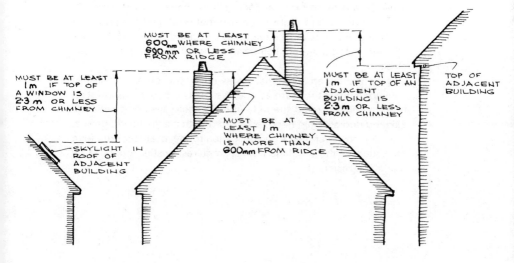

c

Loft conversion

A loft has a potential floor area probably larger than any of the existing rooms of a house and may be an almost ready-made extension to the house. There are firms throughout the country specialising in loft conversions.

It is unlikely that planning permission will be required for a loft conversion since the only addition to the cubic capacity of the house will be any window projections. The conversion will have to comply with the Building Regulations. Some circumstances can make a loft conversion an uneconomic proposition.

One of the first aspects to be considered is whether, by converting a loft into an additional storey, the house will be turned from a two-storey building into a three-storey one. To allow a safe escape route in case of fire, the Building Regulations require the internal stairways, and associated hallways and landings, in houses of three or more storeys to be separated from all other parts of the building by a structure which has a fire resistance of half an hour. Any door which opens from there into a habitable room or a kitchen must also be half an hour fire-resistant and self-closing. In addition, the space associated with a stairway on the ground floor must extend to an external door or must have two exits both of which afford a safe route to an external door, and the structure enclosing the route must have a fire resistance of half an hour with all doors along the route being half an hour fire-resistant and self-closing.

If by forming an additional storey out of the loft, your house is converted into a three-storey one, the local authority may insist on both the existing and the new internal stairways being isolated. Existing doors would need to be fitted with a self-closing device. You can, however, make an application to the local authority for a relaxation of the regulation which requires existing doors to be made fire-resistant.

trussed rafter roof construction

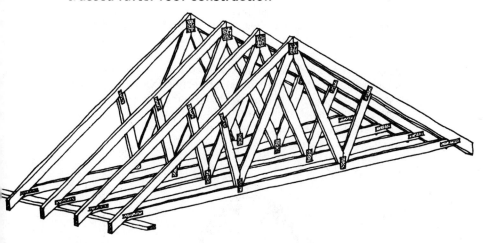

roof structure

First, have a look around the loft to see what obstructions there are. Water storage cisterns and plumbing do not present much of a problem because it is usually a simple matter to have them moved. It is the timbers of the roof structure itself which have to be most carefully considered. If your house was built fairly recently, it is likely that the roof was constructed with trussed rafters. These are made of fairly thin pieces of timber, usually joined with metal plates. Every piece is so dependent on the next that none can be removed without the risk of the remainder collapsing. So to convert a loft with a roof of trussed rafters, a major roof reconstruction will almost certainly be necessary. An architect, building surveyor or architectural consultant should be able to advise you.

The more traditional form of roof construction with rafters and struts presents less of a problem because it is likely that the struts or other supporting timber pieces can be moved to alternative positions without ill effects on the overall stability of the structure.

available height

If you want to create a habitable room in a loft, an important consideration is available height. For a room wholly or partly within a roof, at least half of the room has to have a ceiling height of not less than 2·3 metres (about 7 feet 7 inches). When you measure the existing headroom in the roof space, you should allow at least 200 mm (about 8 inches) for deeper floor joists and for floorboards and for the depth of a ceiling in the new construction. In practice, therefore, the minimum height of a loft to be converted must be 2·5 metres (about 8 feet 2 inches) over at least half the proposed floor area.

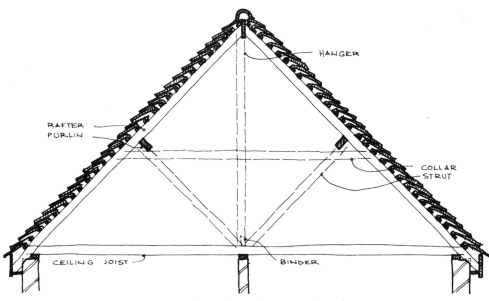

**cross-section of roof space showing
timbers to be removed**

If there is not sufficient floor area with enough headroom within the roof structure as it exists, it may be possible to construct a dormer window to give additional floor area with the required ceiling height.

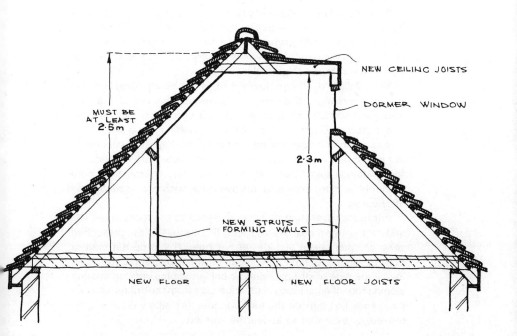

MUST BE AT LEAST 2·5m

NEW CEILING JOISTS

DORMER WINDOW

2·3m

NEW STRUTS FORMING WALLS

NEW FLOOR

NEW FLOOR JOISTS

floor and walls

When the house was built, the loft was intended only as an empty space, so joists were provided for ceiling support only. New, deeper floor joists will have to be provided, capable of withstanding the appropriate extra weight.

The floor surface to be fixed over the new joists must not only be adequate in strength but must also meet the fire precaution regulations.

Depending on the degree of thermal insulation already in the existing roof, a certain amount of additional insulation will probably have to be provided.

If the loft shares a vertical brick wall with an adjacent house, as in the case of semi-detached or terraced property, it will probably be convenient to utilise this party wall as one side of the new room. The wall will probably have to be plastered in order to comply with the regulations which require adequate sound insulation in walls separating dwellings.

New walls in a loft are usually made of timber studding because this is lightweight and easy to fix to the timbers of the roof structure. Some form of access should be provided to the cold water storage cistern in the roof space behind the walls.

You could consider the possibility of making fitted cupboards out of the side spaces. Ask the builder to quote a provisional sum for building in such fittings at the time of the conversion; it would probably be more expensive to have them constructed separately afterwards.

Adequate ventilation must be provided to the room in the loft and, if it is to be a habitable room, there must be the prescribed zone of open space outside the window. If you do not want a dormer window or do not need one for the extra height, you could install the type of skylight window unit which fits into the existing sloping roof. If an existing ventilation pipe from the drains, or a flue pipe, ends just outside the new window, the pipe will have to be moved, or extended to above the window.

stairway

Before you can decide how to arrange the room or rooms you are making in the loft, you have to work out where access to it can be constructed from the floor below, allowing for the amount of space which the staircase will take up.

There are two basic types of stairway to a loft: a permanently fixed staircase and a retractable ladder. A fixed staircase must comply with numerous provisions of the Building Regulations; there are no regulations applying to the ladder type because it is treated as a movable fitting rather than part of the house.

A straight flight is the least expensive fixed stairway, but it is often difficult to fit into a house because it has to be so long. The same type of staircase with the addition of a quarter landing is more easily accommodated. A further variation is to form two quarter landings; this has the effect of turning the stairs through 180 degrees and the staircase can then fit into a relatively small area. A slightly more expensive form of construction, incorporating tapered steps (often referred to as winders by builders), is a good way of saving space because the single step of a quarter landing, for example, can be replaced with three of the tapered kind.

A spiral staircase is the most expensive, and is a luxury item unless you are lucky enough to get hold of a good secondhand one cheaply, which also complies with the Building Regulations. Most builders do not attempt to manufacture such a staircase them-selves, but go to one of the firms which specialise in this kind of work. So even if expense is no object, delivery time may be a deterrent.

The Building Regulations concerned with the general design of a staircase are complicated. There are restrictions on the size of steps and on the steepness of the staircase, which is not allowed to be more than 42 degrees to the floor. The staircase must be at least 600 mm wide if it is a stairway providing access to a bathroom and lavatory only or to one room other than a living room or a kitchen. Otherwise, the stairs must be not less than 800 mm wide. But you should always allow enough width for your furniture to be taken easily up or down the staircase.

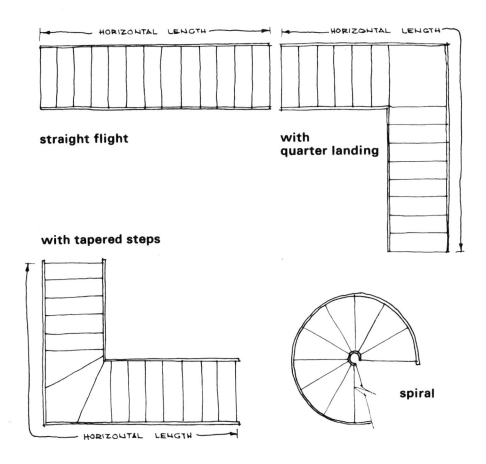

straight flight

**with
quarter landing**

with tapered steps

spiral

Tapered steps have to comply with strict regulations to ensure that they are neither too narrow at the narrowest side, nor too wide at the widest side.

If you know the height between the floor from which the stairs will rise and the level of the new floor at the top, it is possible to work out approximately whether there is sufficient space for the staircase. For a straight flight, add 10 per cent (10 mm for every 100 mm), then measure along the lower floor to see if this space is available. For example, if the height from floor to floor is 2500 mm, the approximate horizontal length required will be 2750 mm. If the staircase is to have a quarter landing, add to this (2750 mm) the length of two sides of the quarter landing: in the case of an 800 mm wide staircase, an addition of 1600 mm, making a total of 4350 mm—nearly $4\frac{1}{2}$ metres (about 14 feet 3 inches).

For a staircase with tapering steps, the total horizontal length required is approximately equal to the overall height from floor to floor.

A spiral staircase requires a circular space having a diameter of twice the width of the stairs plus that of the central post.

headroom
The regulations specify that over any type of fixed staircase there must be a minimum headroom of 2 metres (about 6 feet 7 inches), and complying with this regulation may mean a slight reduction in the floor area above.

guarding of stairway

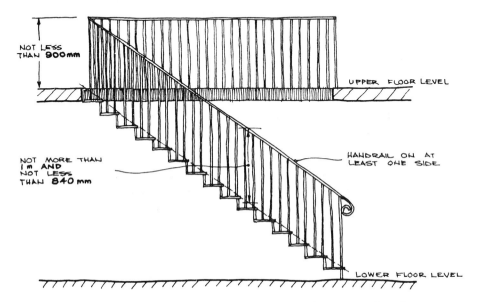

NOT LESS
THAN **900** mm

UPPER FLOOR LEVEL

NOT MORE THAN
I m AND
NOT LESS
THAN **840** mm

HANDRAIL ON AT
LEAST ONE SIDE

LOWER FLOOR LEVEL

The regulations also lay down certain safety precautions for fixed staircases. The stairs must be guarded on each side by a wall or a solid screen, or a balustrade or railings at a height of at least 840 mm (about 2 feet 9 inches) above the treads. Every flight of stairs which rises more than 600 mm (about 2 feet) must have a continuous handrail on one side, ending in a scroll; if the stairs have tapered treads, the handrail must be on the side where the treads are wider. If the width of the stairs is more than 1 metre, a continuous handrail must be provided on both sides. Any landing or area directly overlooking the staircase must be guarded for a height of at least 900 mm (about 3 feet) above the floor level.

If you want a door to the new room at the top of the stairs, you may be tempted to have no landing in order to get as much floor space as possible in the room. However, the Building Regulations stipulate that there must be a landing at the top and bottom of any new stairway, and there must be 2 metre headroom over the landing.

When deciding whether to have a permanent or a retracting stairway, you should bear in mind the use to which the room in the roof is to be put. Retracting stairs usually tend to be rather steep, and some do not have handrails on both sides, aspects which are a hazard for children or elderly people.

The retractable ladder type of stairway in either timber or aluminium can be bought ready-made, or made to measure if the specified dimensions are sent to the ladder manufacturer.

A report on loft ladders was published in *Handyman Which?* August 1974.

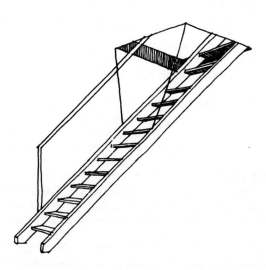

Garages

A garage should not only be large enough for the car which it will accommodate, it must be large enough for the car to be driven in and out, and for the car doors and the boot to be opened easily when the car is inside. For a one-car garage, an internal size of 16 feet by 8 feet (approximately 5 m by 2·5 m) should be regarded as a minimum.

If you are thinking of building a single garage, consider the possibility of wanting a garage to take more than one car at a later date. Make adequate allowance for all the bits and pieces that end up being kept in the garage (such as the lawnmower, tools, wheelbarrow, bicycles, a pram, toys—and maybe a boat in the winter). If you want to have a workbench in the garage, allow enough room to work at it while the car is in the garage.

Even a detached garage is counted as an extension for planning purposes, so if the cubic content of the proposed garage exceeds the 50 cubic metre limit for an extension to the original house, planning permission is required. Planning permission is also required, and may well be refused, if you want the garage or any part of it to be farther forward than the front of the house.

You should find out whether your local authority has any special views on totally obstructing the access way round the side of the house, if this is what building a garage at the side involves. It may mean siting the garage behind the house with a gap of about a metre between the front of the garage and the back wall of the house, or having another door at the back of the garage and allowing a passageway in the garage, even with the car there.

floor and walls

Unlike a floor in a house, there need be no damp-proof membrane in a garage floor, and thermal insulation is not required for the walls or roof of a garage. The walls can be made of lightweight

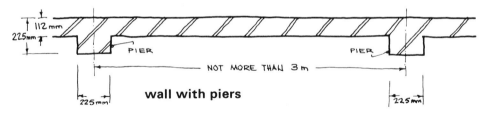

wall with piers

construction such as concrete panels or metal sheets, which do not need a concrete strip foundation.

The thickness of a garage wall not more than 3 metres high, constructed of bricks or blocks, must not be less than 90 mm (about $3\frac{1}{2}$ inches), and if less than 190 mm (about 8 inches), piers (protruding columns) at least 190 mm square must be built in not more than 3 metres apart—as well as at the corners of the building to ensure good stability.

The walls must comply with certain fire precaution regulations. For a detached garage with a floor area of up to 40 square metres, the requirements depend mainly on whether the garage, all or part of it, is less than 2 metres away from the house walls or the nearest boundary. If within 2 metres, the walls must be constructed of non-combustible materials, such as bricks or blocks of concrete panels. (A garage with a floor area of more than 40 square metres is looked on as a storage building and much stricter fire precaution regulations apply; most domestic garages are not as large as this.)

If you want to attach your garage to the house by using an existing house wall as one of the garage walls, that wall must have a specified degree of fire resistance. A brick wall would have this if it is not clad with combustible material. Any door in that wall must be fire-resistant and self-closing, and the threshold has to be at least 100 mm above the level of the garage floor. Windows or any other openings are not permitted in the wall unless fitted with elaborate, fire-resistant shutters actuated by fusible links. Alternatively, any windows, openings or ventilators would have to be bricked up or covered permanently with fire-resistant material. Blocking up an existing window or ventilator which results in depriving a room of its zone of open space or prescribed amount of ventilation will not be allowed unless an alternative window or ventilator can be provided.

If you intend to have an integral garage in the lower half of a two-storey extension, the floor above the garage must be sufficiently fire-resistant. One way of achieving this is by constructing the ceiling of the garage with two sheets of plasterboard.

roof

A pitched roof covered with tiles or slates or corrugated sheets of galvanised steel or asbestos cement complies with the fire precaution regulations for garage roofs. So does asbestos-based roofing felt on boarding provided the required number of layers of the correct grade of roofing felt is used. Translucent roofs are permitted on garages; the siting of the garage determines which grade of translucent materials can be used in order to conform to the fire precaution regulations.

A pitched roof covered with tiles or slates for a garage is attractive but expensive. A pitched roof of corrugated sheets is the cheapest type of roof covering for a garage but the least attractive in appearance.

A flat roof is generally in the middle of the price ranges and can be put on any garage provided the right number of layers and grades of roofing felt are incorporated. Whatever the roof covering, the front wall of a garage can be built up as a parapet to conceal the roof structure and give a pleasant appearance. If planning permission is necessary for your garage, the local authority may insist on a particular type of construction for the roof. Rainwater disposal facilities will almost certainly have to be provided. This means having gutters and a downpipe discharging into a drain or soakaway or a butt.

doors

Garage doors are nowadays often the up-and-over type. These need less space to open than a pair of doors with hinges at the side and will not slam in a gust of wind just as you are about to drive your car into or out of the garage. Up-and-over doors with counterbalance springs (or weights), properly adjusted, require little effort to operate. If made of timber, they are susceptible to distortion through shrinkage and warping. Those of steel or aluminium have the added advantage of being immune to rust and rotting.

car ports

A car port can be made by putting a roof over the space between a detached garage (or other building) and the wall of the house. Alternatively, you can build columns or a new solid wall to support the outer edge of the roof. Prefabricated car ports are available consisting of a translucent roof panel with tubular steel supporting columns.

A car port is defined as a structure of not more than one storey and open on two or more of its sides. A side which includes, or consists of, a door is not counted as open. So if you propose to construct a car port and it is not completely open on at least two sides, it will count as a garage and will have to comply with the appropriate Building Regulations regarding fire precautions for the walls.

Building Regulations apply to the fire resistance of the roofing and the rainwater disposal on a car port, as they do for a garage. If the cubic content of any space enclosed by a car port exceeds the permitted limit for an extension to your house, you will have to get planning permission as well.

converting an integral garage

If your house was built with a garage as an integral part of the building, you can provide yourself with additional living accommodation by converting the garage into a room. Where space permits to construct an alternative garage separately, such an arrangement is likely to be less expensive than retaining the integral garage and having a habitable extension built on. Ask a builder for a rough estimate of the comparative costs of the two alternatives before deciding to convert or to extend.

For a conversion of this sort, you should ask at your local authority offices whether planning permission is required.

The new room converted from the garage must comply with the Building Regulations. A garage floor is unlikely to have a damp-proof membrane, so the new floor will have to incorporate one. The required amount of thermal insulation will have to be provided in all the external walls. Existing cavity walls will therefore have to be plastered, or lined with wallboard. A solid wall may need an inner layer built on to it.

If there is another room above, no additional thermal insulation will be required in the ceiling of the converted room. But if there is a roof space immediately above, thermal insulation will have to be provided in that part of the roof over the new room.

If the new room is going to be a habitable room, there must be a minimum ceiling height of 2·3 metres (about 7 feet 7 inches) over all the floor area. There must also be the prescribed amount of ventilation, and the appropriate zone of open space outside at least one of its windows.

Drawings

When you have decided what your extension should be like, drawings must be prepared for submission to the local authority to show that the proposed scheme complies with the Building Regulations, and to apply for planning permission if necessary. Drawings are also needed to get quotations from builders, and the builder you choose will work from them. In practice, usually one set of detailed drawings is prepared to serve all these purposes.

The drawings do not have to be prepared by a person with professional qualifications: anyone may prepare building drawings for submission to a local authority. But it is not advisable to embark on drawing your own plans unless you have some knowledge not only of drawing, but also of building construction and regulations. The requirements of the local authority may appear straightforward to the initiated but they can be very complex and frustrating to the uninitiated.

It is usual to ask an architect, a building surveyor or an architectural consultant who is trained as a professional draughtsman to prepare the drawings. He should project your ideas rather than his own. An architect may have suggestions for aesthetic improvements, but should not introduce his own ideas without your agreement. The architect, surveyor or consultant will know what the current regulations and local requirements are, and what must (and what need not) be shown on drawings in order to get approval from the appropriate authorities.

If you have not already been in touch with an architect, a builder may suggest someone who could be asked to prepare the drawings, or he may offer to get them done. Not many builders prepare drawings themselves.

Whoever prepares the drawings, you should make sure that they show your requirements precisely and correctly. If you do not understand anything on a drawing, ask for an explanation.

For an extension to a house, the drawings consist of a floor plan (or plans of each floor level if the scheme involves more than one storey of the building), elevations (which are views of the various

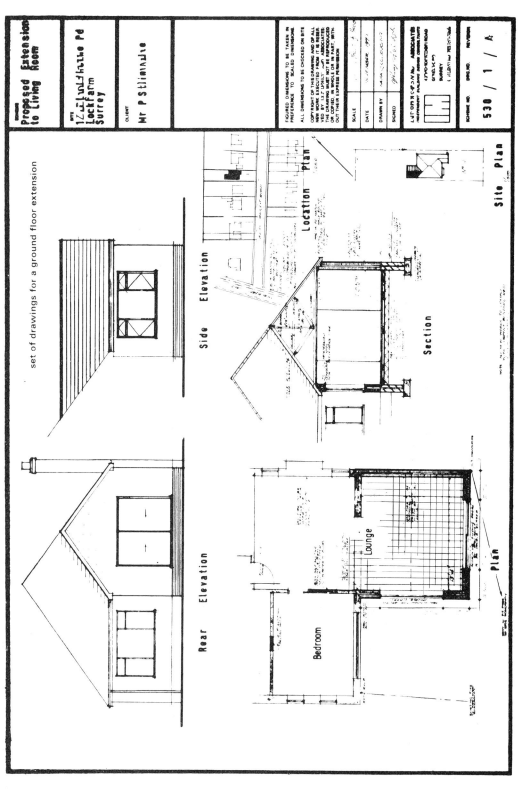

set of drawings for a ground floor extension

Side Elevation

Location Plan

Section

Site Plan

Rear Elevation

Bedroom

Lounge

Plan

Proposed Extension to Living Room

1Z̄ Lunlkhbe Pd Lochfarm Surrey

CLIENT

Mr P Stliniaulve

FIGURED DIMENSIONS TO BE TAKEN IN PREFERENCE TO SCALED DIMENSIONS.

ALL DIMENSIONS TO BE CHECKED ON SITE

COPYRIGHT OF THIS DRAWING AND OF ALL NEW WORK EXECUTED FROM IT IS RESERVED BY I.T UNWIN AND ASSOCIATES. THE DRAWING MUST NOT BE REPRODUCED OR COPIED IN WHOLE OR IN PART, WITHOUT THEIR EXPRESS PERMISSION

SCALE	
DATE	
DRAWN BY	
SIGNED	

LI.T OP.Y TC.IP.D/N' No. ASSOCIATES
INDEPENDENT BUILDING DESIGN CONSULTANTS
GRID.HC.IM
SURREY
(VILDNTI and PES.DP.Rdd

SCHEME NO.   DRG NO.   REVISION

530 / 1 / A

EXTENDING YOUR HOUSE

page 18   grants for house improvement

From 15 August 1977, the eligible expense limits for grants are increased to the following maximum amounts:

for an intermediate grant	£1200, plus £1500 for associated repair or replacement work
for an improvement grant	£5000

The maximum percentage of the eligible expense which can be given as a grant remains the same: 50 per cent generally, but 60 per cent or 75 per cent in certain designated areas.

The rateable value limit below which a property qualifies for an improvement grant is now £400 in Greater London, £225 elsewhere in England or Wales.

August 1977

a/s 75

sides of the building), a cross-section through the building. Usually a plan is included showing the position of the property in relation to the surrounding district and also a plan showing the proposed extension in relation to the house and the remainder of the property. Sometimes partial enlargements of plans, elevations or sections are also included, to show some particular aspects of the scheme in detail. The drawings should contain sufficient detail for a builder to be able to give a quotation and use them when carrying out the work. For most house extensions, all the drawings go on to one sheet of paper or perhaps two at the most.

specification

In addition to drawings, both the local authority and the builder will need a detailed specification. This may be a written document relating to the particular drawings, specifying exactly the materials to be used and the way in which the work is to be carried out. It describes everything in detail, from the proportions of cement, sand and ballast in the concrete for the foundations, to the way in which the roof tiles should be fixed. Not all, but many of these details are required by the local authority, and the builder will base his quotation on the specification. You should therefore have decided by this stage on details such as the kind of bricks, types of window, roof covering and floors, major installations, plumbing and general finish.

The specification is drawn up by the architect, the building surveyor or architectural consultant, and if not part of his overall fee, he will probably charge you on an hourly basis for it.

For a simple extension, instead of a separate specification, details may be written in on the drawings in the form of construction notes. These also point out how the scheme complies with the various requirements of the Building Regulations or of the local planning authority.

The local authority

If you are a ratepayer, the body to whom you pay rates is your local authority. Someone who is not a ratepayer can find out which is the appropriate local authority by asking at the nearest main post office or public library or citizens' advice bureau.

Before deciding to go ahead with a scheme to make substantial improvements to your property, you may want to know by how much your rates are likely to be increased. It might be possible to get an answer once you have some detailed drawings showing the proposed scheme. Look up the appropriate valuation office of the Inland Revenue in your telephone directory, or ask for the valuation officer's address at the office where you pay your rates. If you send a copy of the drawings to your local valuation officer with an appropriate covering letter, he may be prepared to give you an indication of any likely increase in the rateable value as a result of carrying out such a scheme. There is, however, no obligation on his part to do so, and any figures that he may give at this stage must be treated only as a guide.

getting planning permission

If your proposed extension does not fall within the permitted development for your property, you must obtain planning permission from your local planning authority.

In England and Wales, the county council (or metropolitan county council) is the planning authority for the relevant county, but most of the general planning matters are delegated to the respective district councils. For practical purposes, any planning enquiry should, in the first place, be addressed to your district council (or metropolitan district council); in London, to the borough council.

The local planning office may be part of the engineer and surveyor's department of the local authority; it may be part of the architect's department, or be a separate department on its own. Records of all planning applications made, ordnance survey maps showing the district in detail, and development plan maps showing the council's future planning policy for the area, are available for inspection at the office.

Making an application for planning permission is a fairly simple procedure. Anyone can make the application: it will be treated in the same way whether made by an architect or a surveyor or an architectural consultant, or a builder, or a private individual.

If you are going to make the application, you should telephone or go to the planning office and ask for the necessary forms. The staff there will, if you want, show you how to fill them in. Many planning offices issue guidance notes which say exactly what drawings and other documents are required, and how many copies have to be submitted. These notes are useful when you return home and cannot quite remember what you were told.

If you have any doubt about whether a planning application is required, it is better to submit an application. (Or you can write a letter to the local planning authority asking whether what is proposed needs an application for planning permission.) The local planning authority will soon say if planning permission is not required for your scheme. The expense of submitting an application is minimal—extra copies of the drawings, which you will anyway be needing for other purposes, and the time taken to fill in the required number of copies of the application form.

The documents required for an application consist of forms and drawings of the proposed scheme, giving a description of the work for which permission is required. There is a standardised application form drawn up by the Department of the Environment which local authorities are encouraged to adopt, but each authority can use its own version. Some authorities require a great many written answers on their application form, others ask only a few questions and rely for details on the drawings. Most authorities require the form to be completed in triplicate with a set of drawings for each copy.

With the form is a certificate stating that the person making the application is the owner of the land to which the application relates, or is the tenant. If this is not the case, a different certificate has to be completed, stating that the applicant has notified the owner of the land (a form for doing this is provided with the application form). You would have to complete this certificate if you were contemplating buying a property with the intention of altering it. There is nothing to stop anyone applying for planning permission relating to land he does not own or of which he is not the tenant, and this notice allows the owner of land for which someone else has submitted a planning application to make an objection to the planning authority if he wishes to do so.

The forms, complete with drawings, should be taken or sent to the local planning office. The planning officer dealing with the application may need further information from you in order to clarify some particular points. He then passes the application on to the council, usually with a recommendation for approval or rejection.

A council generally meets once a month. Most councils have a planning committee which meets more frequently for the purpose of considering planning applications. You can telephone the planning office to find out when the next meeting is, and by when applications should be submitted. Many committees are empowered to make a final decision on applications without reference to the full council. In most cases, a decision will be made by the planning committee or council at its first available meeting.

A written notice of approval or rejection is then sent to the applicant. If approval is given subject to conditions, the conditions are listed, together with the reasons for their imposition. If a rejection notice is issued, the reasons for the rejection are listed on the form.

The length of time between submitting an application and getting a decision is usually between five and eight weeks. If no decision is reached within two months of the date of an application (in some circumstances, three months), the local planning authority should seek the written consent of the applicant to extend the period. If the applicant does not agree, the application is automatically rejected.

An aggrieved applicant may, within six months, appeal to the Department of the Environment (in Wales, the Welsh Office), giving reasons why he considers that the conditions attached to an approval are unreasonable, or in the case of a rejection, why he considers that an approval should have been granted. An appeal may also be made against a failure to give a decision in time or against an authority's ruling that the proposed extension is not permitted development and so needs an application for planning permission.

A booklet called *Planning appeals: a guide to procedure* is issued by the Department of the Environment. It is obtainable from the Department and from the Welsh Office, and explains what disappointed applicants can do to find out whether there is a chance of success if they appeal, and the procedure for appeals. It may be advisable to have professional advice.

If planning permission is granted, the work must be carried out in accordance with the approved plans. Planning permission remains valid for five years (unless any other period is stated in the approval notice). If by that time the work has not been started, permission must be sought anew.

listed building consent

Listed building consent is obtained from the local planning authority.

If an application for planning permission has been made to the local authority for work to be done to a listed building and permission granted, this can also operate as listed building consent. If planning permission is not necessary for the proposed work, listed building consent must be obtained before the work is commenced. The local planning office will supply the appropriate application forms. There is a right of appeal to the Department of the Environment or the Welsh Office against the refusal of listed building consent.

getting Building Regulations approval

The Building Regulations specify in considerable detail the written notices, plans, and other particulars which must be submitted to the local authority by any person who intends to execute any work to a building, including any structural alteration or extension.

For any work to a partially exempted building, it is not necessary to comply with all of the Building Regulations unless by doing the work the building will cease to be exempt. But some regulations are likely to apply in any case. (The classes of partially exempted buildings and the regulations which apply to them are specified in a schedule to the Building Regulations.)

To obtain Building Regulations approval, notice has to be given and plans deposited at the local building control office (or building inspector's office), which is usually part of the engineer and surveyor's department of the local authority, and is often in the same building as the local planning office. It is headed by a chief building control officer, who has working with him building control officers (in some places still called building inspectors), each responsible for a certain area of the local authority's territory.

A building control officer can advise on any queries arising on the interpretation of the Building Regulations. You should telephone his office to find out the best time of day to contact him personally; he is not always available there, since the bulk of his time is spent examining applications submitted, and visiting the building operations in progress in his area.

If the building control officer was employed by the council when your house was originally built, he will probably have more knowledge of its construction than you have yourself, and will certainly have a good knowledge of such items as subsoil conditions and drainage facilities in the vicinity of your property. So if you now wish to make alterations or extensions to it, and are not sure about the drainage or foundations of your house, you could ask him for information.

The building control office supplies the two copies of the formal notification required for Building Regulations approval. Many local authorities issue free guidance notes. These are often reprints of the relevant schedule in the Building Regulations, and can be helpful if you are making the notification yourself.

Drawings of the proposed work are required in duplicate. Some authorities require one set of drawings on linen-wove paper or other durable material. The number of questions to be answered on the form varies with different authorities; many take the view that, since constructional details must be shown clearly on the drawings, there is no need to have them also explained in writing on the form; others consider that constructional details are better clarified on a question-and-answer basis. If there is any doubt about the proposal as indicated by the form or on the drawings, the applicant or his representative is asked for further information. If the building control officer is satisfied that the proposed work would not contravene any of the regulations, he recommends the application for approval.

If a reparable error has been made in the proposals, or if part of the scheme does not comply with the regulations but can be amended easily to do so, most building control officers contact the applicant or his representative and ask for the proposals to be amended. It is unusual for a properly presented Building Regulations notification to be rejected without the person who submitted it being consulted first. Many of the regulations are very complicated and their interpretation often varies from one local authority to another.

In some circumstances it is worth asking for a regulation to be relaxed—for instance, the one regarding the 2·3 metre ceiling height if all the existing rooms in your cottage have ceilings less than this height. There is an official form on which to apply for a relaxation. You have to produce convincing reasons why the particular regulation should be relaxed or dispensed with.

Building Regulations approval can be withheld only if the proposed work would not comply with one or more of the regulations—unlike planning permission which can be refused at the discretion of a local authority in the light of its development policy.

Few local authority councils require Building Regulations notifications to be brought to a full council meeting; most allow their own planning and development committees to give final decisions. Many local authorities have further delegated this power to the appropriate chief officer who can issue approval notices on the recommendation of his building officers. There is generally not as long a wait as there can be for planning permission. The prescribed period within which a decision should be given is five weeks; this can be extended to two months in certain circumstances.

The Building Regulations state that the person carrying out the work must notify the local authority at certain specified stages so that the building control officer can inspect the ongoing work and have tests made where necessary. Most authorities send with their approval notice a series of postcards, addressed to the appropriate officer, to be completed and sent to him at the relevant stages of the work, as indicated on each card. If you are employing a builder, you should give him these cards before he starts any work.

If planning permission is granted subject to changes in the proposed scheme which affect the design or the construction or the siting of the building, you have to submit the amended drawings for fresh Building Regulations approval. (In some cases, it may be vice versa.)

inner London
The Building Regulations do not cover building operations in the inner London area; instead, the London Building Acts and the various by-laws made under them apply.

A builder must give the district surveyor in whose district the work is to take place at least two clear days' notice before commencing work. It is the builder's responsibility to give this notice, on a form supplied by the district surveyor's office. The district surveyor may require drawings and other particulars.

The district surveyor does not issue a formal notice of approval, but the work can go ahead if he raises no queries within the two days. In order to avoid possible delay at the point when you are ready to start work, you or your architect can send particulars of the scheme to the district surveyor in advance. Any further details can then be dealt with in good time and agreed by the district surveyor so that when the builder is ready to start all he has to do is to send in the formal notice.

It is the job of the district surveyor to supervise a building operation and the GLC is paid a fee for his services, based on the cost of the work supervised. When the cost of the work does not exceed £50, the fee is £5; when the work costs between £50 and £100, the fee is £6; between £100 and £1000, it is £6 plus £1.50 for every £100 over the first £100; between £1000 and £5000, it is £19.50 plus 50p for every £100 over the first £1000. The builder is directly responsible for paying the district surveyor but may try to recover the amount from you, unless the contract between the builder and you says otherwise.

In the inner London boroughs, sanitation and drainage are the responsibility of each local authority and not of the district surveyor. Therefore, if a proposed scheme involves any drainage work, you must apply to the local authority for approval for such work by completing a form much the same as that for a Building Regulations notification in any other part of the country. An approval notice must then be obtained from that authority before any work is actually begun.

The contract

Some people feel that they know a local builder so well that they are prepared to let him carry out a house extension without bothering to enter into a written agreement, and are satisfied for the work to be done on the basis of mutual trust. This arrangement should be the exception rather than the rule. Even for a small job, it is strongly advisable to have a written agreement showing exactly what work is to be carried out, the conditions on which it is to be carried out and for what price. This can be done by the exchange of letters confirming what was discussed, but it is usually better to have a formal contract.

There are two basic types of building contracts. In one, referred to generally as a lump sum or fixed price contract, an overall sum is agreed to cover the job as specified. This amount is known as the contract price. The builder will charge you this unless a clause is included to cover fluctuations in the cost of materials after the date of signing the contract. Many builders are nowadays reluctant to quote a fixed price when the cost of materials could increase substantially during the progress of the work. Instead of a builder quoting what could well be an inflated fixed price to allow for all possible increases, a fluctuations clause can be included in a fixed price contract. This allows the builder to calculate an accurate quotation but to charge you subsequently with any justified increase in the cost of materials.

In the other type of contract, no sums are agreed in advance. The contract merely states that the builder will carry out any work as required by the person employing him, and will charge for what the work costs the builder, plus an agreed percentage or a sum to cover the builder's overheads and profit. This type of contract is not very satisfactory for an employer because, since there is no incentive, there is no obligation on the part of the builder to use the most economical or most suitable materials, and the wages bill for the work may be high.

If drawings and a specification have been prepared, a lump sum contract is generally more suitable for an extension scheme.

If you have already consulted an architect, surveyor or other consultant, he will advise you about the type and content of a contract to suit your circumstances.

An architect will probably offer you the RIBA's printed form of agreement for minor building works. The standard conditions on which the agreement is based are set out and the form just has to be filled in with names, dates and figures. Anyone can use the RIBA form of agreement; copies can be bought from the RIBA price 32p for one copy (plus 15p postage).

Other organisations produce similar ready-made forms of contract. An architectural or similar consultant will prepare a building agreement for a small fee, even if you are not engaging him to supervise the job.

If you do not put forward any form of contract, a builder's quotation usually contains his standard terms and conditions. They should be read carefully because they would form the basis of a contract if his tender is accepted and there is no other formal contract.

Alternatively, you could type out a contract with its conditions, yourself, in duplicate. A solicitor is not required but is advisable if the extent of the job justifies the additional safeguard and expense.

The following are clauses which could be adopted for a lump sum contract:

1. The builder shall carry out and complete the work in strict accordance with the drawing and specification attached hereto, in a good workmanlike manner and to the reasonable satisfaction of the employer for the sum of . . . . (£ . . . . . .)

2. Possession of the site will be given to the builder on. . . . . He shall commence work immediately after such possession, shall regularly proceed with the work, and shall complete the work by . . . . , subject only to changes agreed according to the provision of clause 6 below.

3. If the builder shall fail or neglect to complete the work on or before the date in clause 2, he agrees to pay the employer (by way of damages, and not by way of penalty) the sum of . . . . for every week or part of a week during which the completion is delayed.

4. The builder shall, within fourteen days of completing the work, and at his own expense, remove all tools, surplus materials and rubbish from the site and leave it in a clean and tidy condition.

5. The builder shall comply with all prevailing rules, regulations, laws and by-laws relating to the works; he shall pay all fees legally due in connection with them and shall be responsible for giving all necessary notices, and arranging for inspections to take place.

6. No variation to the work described in clause 1 shall invalidate the contract, but any such variation, whether by addition, omission, or substitution, together with the cost and effect on the date of completion, shall be agreed in writing between the employer and the builder before the variation is carried out, and the contract price stated in clause 1 and the date of completion stated in clause 2 shall be altered accordingly.

(If you decide to adopt a fluctuations clause, the following could be added after clause 6: '6(a) The contract price stated in clause 1 was based on the cost of materials as at . . . (date) and shall be adjusted by adding any additional costs incurred or deducting any costs saved by the builder by reason of any increase or decrease after that date in the prices of materials or commodities detailed in the attached photocopies and summarised below . . . (list).')

7. The builder shall take out insurance indemnifying the employer for all loss, claims or proceedings arising out of or in the course of the execution of the contract, and for all costs and charges incurred in relation to the investigation or settling of such claims.

8. The builder shall be responsible for insuring the work in the joint names of himself and the employer for loss or damage by fire for the full value from the date of commencement until possession is taken.

9. The builder shall make good at his own expense any damage caused by him, his agents or his employees or by any subcontractor.

10. The builder shall make good at his own expense any defects, shrinkages or other faults which may appear within six months from the completion of the works arising from materials or workmanship not in accordance with the contract.

11. The following prices for execution of work of the supply of materials are for payment to the parties stated:

provisional items

PC sums

12. The employer shall pay to the builder 95 per cent of the sum mentioned in clause 1, or such other sum as may have been agreed in accordance with clause 6, upon the submission by the builder of the final account following the completion of the work, the balance to be paid by the employer to the builder at the expiration of six months from the date of completion of the work or when all defects have been made good in accordance with clause 10, whichever is the later.

13. The employer and the builder agree that should any dispute or difference arise between them out of the work, either party shall give to the other written notice of such dispute or difference and at the same time shall refer the matter to an arbitrator agreed by both parties, whose decision shall be final and binding on both parties.

the clauses

Important in clause 1 is that if the builder does not complete the work to the reasonable satisfaction of the employer, he commits a breach of contract and lays himself open to a claim for damages. The employer, as a layman, may be at some disadvantage here since his lack of technical knowledge may make it difficult for him to judge the standard of workmanship. If an architectural consultant or a building surveyor is going to supervise the work, the clause could stipulate that the work must be carried out to his reasonable satisfaction.

For clause 2, factors which could be agreed as reasonable cause for delay would be unseasonably bad weather or specified parts or materials unexpectedly becoming unobtainable—for instance, if the only supplier goes bankrupt.

Clause 3 is intended to ensure that the work is completed by the agreed date or that you are paid something in compensation if it is not. This sum is referred to as 'damages' rather than a penalty; courts do not permit penalties, and if an argument with your builder about the time for completion finished up in court, you would not be allowed to charge the builder a penalty for failing to complete on time. But you could reasonably withhold an amount for damages if a delay in completion caused additional expenses such as hotel, garaging or furniture storage bills. You have to estimate beforehand how much a delay would genuinely cost you, so that a figure can be put into the contract, to be agreed by the builder.

The provisions of clause 6 should be observed most strictly. The lack of written agreement of the cost or value of variations to contracted work is the commonest reason for arguments between builders and employers after work is completed. In the event of any variation—however small—you should, having first discussed the details with the builder, confirm the variation in duplicate, including the amended contract price and completion date, and each keep one of the copies, signed by both. This procedure may seem unnecessary at the time but it could save a lot of trouble later.

If a fluctuations clause 6(a) is included, the builder will, on completion of the work, be allowed to claim any extra amounts which he pays for those materials which are listed in the clause. The builder should have obtained quotations from his suppliers at the outset and attached photocopies of these to the contract. When submitting his final account, he will have to submit also photocopies of invoices to justify any increases in costs.

Clauses 7 and 8 refer to the insurance the builder should have. Most builders have a blanket policy which covers all the projects on which they are working at any one time. Check that the builder has current third party liability insurance and employer's liability insurance. Fire insurance for the extension should be the builder's responsibility until you move in. The insurance policy should be in your joint names. Otherwise, if the building is completely destroyed by fire, for instance, and the insurance company pays the insured sum to the builder, he could abscond without handing any over to you. An alternative is for you to extend your existing house insurance policy to include fire damage to the new work. You should in any case inform your insurers that you are extending your house, before the work starts.

Clause 10 has the effect of asking a builder to guarantee both his workmanship and the materials used. The period stated could be less than six months, but a builder who will not agree to a minimum of three months is not worth employing.

Where applicable, clause 11 would be followed by a table listing what are referred to as provisional items and prime cost sums. Provisional items are optional features or fittings which, at the beginning of the scheme, you are not sure whether you want to have (if they are eventually not carried out, the appropriate sum should be deducted from the final price for the job). A provisional item can also be work which the builder will have to carry out but an accurate assessment of the extent of the work is impossible until some work has started—for example, work in an inaccessible part of the building such as the inside of a roof.

Prime cost (or PC) sums refer to work that will probably be subcontracted (such as the electrical work and plumbing). A sum is reserved but you will be charged their actual cost, which may turn out to be more, or less. You can yourself quote the amounts to be allocated for payment to specified firms or individuals for

D

supplying a particular piece of equipment. The reason for having prime cost items in the contract is to make sure that they are included in the overall price for the whole job. If you know the cost of a fitting that you want, you can fill in the sum, otherwise the builder should.

An example of what might be included in this clause is as follows:

provisional items	cost £	contractor or supplier
concrete path and paved area as shown on the drawings		

PC sums

bathroom fittings:	(you can specify	Tinpan Ironmongers Ltd
electrical work:	if you know	Sparks and Company
heating installation:	what you want)	Pipe Bros Limited

The column nominating contractors or suppliers can be filled in by you or by the builder who is quoting. If you want any special fittings (an XYZ fireplace, for instance), you should tell the builder and he will allow PC sums accordingly. He will include a sum in his quotation for all the plumbing which is obviously necessary but a circular bath or gold-plated taps would be PC sums.

If you subsequently change your mind about a prime cost item, this constitutes a variation to the contract and the consequent adjustment in price should be agreed between you and the builder.

Decoration of the new structure, either inside or outside, is usually dealt with as a provisional or prime cost item, so that you get an approximate idea of the likely cost, the actual amount depending on the wallpaper or paint or other items you finally choose to have. Even if you intend to do the decorating yourself, certain items should be specified, such as priming of woodwork to ensure that it is adequately protected from weather during construction.

If there are many provisional items or PC sums, it may be better to list them on a separate sheet of paper attached to the contract, and to refer to the list in the relevant clause of the contract. If you yourself buy any items for which a PC sum has been allowed, those PC sums should be deleted from the contract. You have to pay value added tax on the amounts you pay direct to a supplier, but if the builder buys items for you, he will be able to reclaim the VAT.

Clause 12 states the method by which the builder is to be paid. Since the builder has agreed to carry out and complete the work for the sum of £XXX, this sum is not due until the work is completed. Many builders ask for stage payments, which means that a specified percentage of the contract price is payable at certain stages of the work.

If the arrangement is to pay at specified stages of the work (the foundations completed, walls up, roof on), the payment should be a percentage of the contract price, not based on the valuation of the work done so far: unless you have some knowledge of building costs you will be unable to make an accurate assessment of the value of the work completed at each stage. Do not make the first payment until the builder starts work. If no interim payments are made, and the builder has to borrow to finance the work or materials, he will pass the borrowing costs on to you by quoting a higher price for the job. Whatever arrangement is chosen, it should be stated clearly in the contract. It is always wise to stipulate that you will retain 5 per cent of the total price for a specified period after completion. For an extension, this is usually between three and six months.

Clause 13 allows for the nomination of an independent arbitrator in the event of any dispute between the builder and yourself. You can agree that such an arbitrator should be appointed by an independent body, such as the Institute of Arbitrators, or if you prefer, you can nominate a particular person as arbitrator: for example, a surveyor or an architect or an architectural consultant (check beforehand that he is willing to be nominated).

Some contracts include a clause allowing for the contract to be terminated in certain circumstances—if either you or the builder become bankrupt, for example, or if you fail to make any agreed interim payment to the builder.

If a builder does not like the terms of your proposed contract, he can either refuse to quote for the work or suggest amendments. He may, for instance, suggest that a clause is included whereby he has to be paid within fourteen days of presenting his bill; or a clause to allow him to employ subcontractors with your written consent (he would remain responsible for the work of the subcontractors).

Quotations

Before entering into a binding contract with one builder, it is advisable to get quotations from two or three independent builders. The procedure for getting quotations is professionally known as obtaining tenders: selected builders are each invited to tender a price for carrying out the work.

If you have engaged an architect or surveyor, he will undertake the business of obtaining tenders as part of his normal service, and will advise on which to choose.

Many people, eager to obtain quotations as soon as the drawings and other details have been prepared and appropriate applications submitted to their local authority, ask builders for quotations straightaway before the necessary approvals have been obtained from the local authority. This is not a good policy, because the local authority may insist on certain amendments being made. Furthermore, there is a chance that the application may be rejected. Preparation of a quotation for building work generally takes up quite a lot of a builder's time, so if the builders who have been invited to quote for the work have been put to a lot of trouble unnecessarily, the customer is not only unpopular with the builders involved, but may find that those builders are not prepared to give another quotation for an amended version of the scheme.

If you have already approached two or three firms for preliminary estimates, the fact that they are then asked for a quotation does not come as a surprise. But if you now want others to tender, you should, both as a matter of courtesy and in order to avoid wasting documents, get in touch with them and find out whether they are interested before formally asking them to tender.

You should then write to each of the selected builders enclosing the drawings and specification and your proposed contract. For a more complex extension, a schedule of prices may be advisable. A schedule lists all the items that will be required, leaving a space opposite each for the builder to fill in what he will charge or at what rate he will charge. Such a breakdown of prices minimises argument if there are any subsequent variations. An architect, building surveyor or architectural consultant will prepare such a schedule for you. (A more elaborate version of a schedule of prices is a bill of quantities prepared by a quantity surveyor. A bill of quantities is unlikely to be required for a straightforward house extension.)

Your letter to each builder should include a list of the enclosures, the date by which tenders must be submitted, what arrangements the builder should make for inspecting the site, and a request for acknowledgment of the letter. If timing is particularly important (for instance, having the work done while you are away, or before the winter), make this clear from the start. It might be wise to add a phrase to the effect that neither the lowest tender nor any particular tender will necessarily be accepted.

The following is an example:

13 June 1977

Dear Sir

I am writing to invite you to tender for the construction of a single-storey extension to my house at the above address.

I enclose one copy of the drawings, specification, and the proposed contract, and shall be pleased if you will let me have your tender not later than the last day of this month.

You can start work on the site on or after 1 August. Please let me know when you could start and how long it would take you to complete.

You may come and inspect the site any time during the next ten days, but I shall be grateful if you will telephone me in advance to arrange a mutually convenient appointment.

I would appreciate your acknowledgment of receipt of this letter and enclosures.

Yours faithfully

M. J. Seaton

The date by which tenders are requested should allow enough time for a builder to prepare his price. Three weeks is a minimum; four weeks would be more reasonable. Having stated a date, you should stick to it, and any builder who does not submit a tender by the date specified should not be considered. Nor should one who has not come to inspect the site.

With his quotation and proposed time schedule, each builder should send back all the documents you sent him, having filled in the spaces where necessary for provisional items and prime cost sums in the contract, but without completing the contract itself. The sums quoted for prime cost items provide a basis for comparing the total prices submitted by different builders. You can tell, for instance, whether the £200 difference between two quotations is due only to different allowances for the same PC items.

If you sent a schedule of prices, this should also be completed by the builders.

The quotations received may vary considerably. Each tender is affected by the particular builder's overheads—office expenses, running costs of lorries and machinery, wages—and profit margin. A builder who is short of work will perhaps submit a low price because he is prepared to do no more than break even solely to keep his men employed. On the other hand, a builder with plenty of work may submit a high price because he wants his tender to be accepted only if he can make a substantial profit.

If you receive any tenders in advance of the date you have given as a deadline, do not disclose the prices submitted to any other builders who have not yet sent in their tenders.

Generally, the lowest tender is accepted unless there is any reason either to doubt the validity of the offer (if, for instance, the builder in a letter to you has used an ambiguous phrase), or to doubt the integrity or competence of the builder submitting it. If you consider all the tenders too high, you are free not to accept any.

When you have decided to accept one cf the tenders, two copies of the contract should be dated and signed by both the builder and yourself, and your signatures witnessed. The builder and yourself should each retain a copy.

One copy of the drawings and any other documents should be attached to each contract and signed by both the builder and yourself, with an endorsement:

'This is one of the documents referred to in the contract between
. . . .(builder) and . . . .
(employer) signed by them on . . . . 1977.

When you have accepted one of the tenders, it is courteous to advise the other builders in a short letter, thanking each builder for tendering and listing the prices quoted (without linking them to the builders' names). Knowing other prices may assist a builder on future occasions. It is wise, however, not to send your letter until after you have signed a formal contract with one of the firms.

Professional supervision

The normal services of an architect or surveyor include two or three visits to the site while the work is being carried out. If you want him to supervise more, he will charge on a time basis. If you engaged an architect, surveyor or architectural consultant to prepare the drawings and any other documents, it is worth considering appointing him or his firm to supervise the builder, to deal with any difficulties that arise and make the necessary spot decisions. Before deciding to do so, you should enquire what the charge will be.

Straightforward building work being done by an established and experienced firm of builders may not need supervision.

If you decide to ask an architect, a building surveyor, or an architectural consultant to supervise the work, your contract with the builder should clearly define the extent of your representative's responsibilities. He should visit the site regularly as the work proceeds to ensure generally that the scheme is carried out in strict accordance with the contract, and that payment is not made at any stage unless the appropriate work has been done. If any variation becomes necessary, he can advise on this. For instance, what to do if a supplier fails to deliver—choose alternative goods? wait? change the design to avoid the need?

The builder must send the requisite notices to the local authority during the progress of the work (a clause in the contract emphasises this) so that the local authority's building control officer can visit the site when certain stages of construction have been completed in order to inspect the foundation trenches, concrete foundations, damp-proofing, drains, roof construction, hearths for heating and cooking appliances. He will have tests carried out on any new drainage work.

If he is not satisfied with any materials or workmanship, he will require the builder to make good as necessary. This should not give rise to any expense to you: if the building control officer is not satisfied with any materials or worksmanship, the work in question would also not be to your satisfaction, and not to put it right would therefore constitute a breach of the contract.

Almost any structure, from a coal bunker to a complete house, is nowadays available in prefabricated form.

There are specialist firms who manufacture prefabricated garages, car ports, ground floor house extensions, bathroom units, garden sheds and greenhouses. These manufacturers advertise regularly in the national and local newspapers and in the popular monthly magazines for householders and do-it-yourself enthusiasts. In most cases, the return of a completed coupon is all that is required to obtain an attractive free colour brochure showing a wide range of sizes, materials and colours, usually complete with price lists and order form. (A few firms send a representative as well as a brochure.)

If you get brochures from a number of manufacturers about their prefabricated structures, compare what is offered by each, and study their price lists carefully. You should be able to find out what types of roof are available (solid, pvc, glass), whether gutters are included in the basic price, whether there are alternative types of floor at any extra cost, whether an assembly service is provided, what delivery charges there might be, how long it will all take, and what any guarantee covers.

Each manufacturer has showgrounds where the entire range of his prefabricated products can be seen assembled so that a prospective purchaser can inspect them before deciding to complete an order form. Showgrounds are staffed by the manufacturer's representatives who should be able to answer customers' questions on any points not made clear in the brochures. The locations of a manufacturer's showgrounds are listed in his brochure; some manufacturers have only one or two sites, some have more than thirty throughout the country.

The factor which influences most people when choosing between a purpose-built structure and a prefabricated one is cost. At first glance, the prefabricated structure is the less expensive. But the total cost of a prefabricated building is rarely the basic price quoted in a brochure. To this figure may have to be added optional extras, such as extra windows or doors, perhaps gutters and rainwater pipes, fire-resistant wall panels. The cost of a proper base and perhaps of rainwater disposal to meet the requirements of the local authority must be added and, finally, the cost of erection allowed for. Only one or two prefabricated building manufacturers provide a complete service. Most are concerned only with selling a kit of component parts. Even so, a prefabricated structure can be less expensive than the equivalent purpose-built structure—this is the big advantage.

Planning permission and Building Regulations approval, where applicable, must be obtained from the local authority before a prefabricated building is put up. It is wise not to place a firm order until you know that your application to the local authority has been approved.

Manufacturers of prefabricated buildings supply typical drawings of their structures, either free or at a nominal charge, for submission to the local authority, but these drawings may have to be amended, or even redrawn in more detail, to show whether the proposed building complies with all requirements. Check in the brochure whether plans are supplied (a firm may say that it will not issue plans until you have given a firm order) and whether applications to the local authority are handled by the firm. Some manufacturers of prefabricated structures require either the whole or part of the payment to be made with the order—it may be several weeks or months before delivery takes place.

Most manufacturers of prefabricated extensions leave you to make your own arrangements for assembly; some provide names and addresses of builders whom they recommend.

Unless you have enough enthusiasm and spare time, and some skill, it is likely that you will need to employ a builder to do at least some of the work, such as constructing the foundations, assembling the prefabricated parts, and providing rainwater disposal facilities. Electrical installations and plumbing, internal or external decorations involve additional work. Find out in advance what the builder will charge. He should be able to give you an estimate based on the brochure. A formal agreement should be made between yourself and the person or firm who is going to carry out the work.

Problems can arise if any faults develop after assembly. Some manufacturers of prefabricated structures offer guarantees to cover faulty materials; others do not. But if, for example, gaps appear between wall panels, the cause could be badly constructed foundations or defective wall panels or faulty erection. If two or more parties have been involved in the job, it could be difficult to hold any one individual or firm responsible. For this reason, try to arrange with a builder that he orders and erects the prefabricated unit. Then he alone deals with the manufacturer, not you. He, if he accepts the job, is responsible to you that it is satisfactory.

garages

Any garage must be erected on a base which conforms to the local authority's requirements. The surface of the base must be level, because an uneven base can cause the panels of a prefabricated concrete garage to crack after assembly, and manufacturers do not accept responsibility for components damaged in this way. A few prefabricated garage manufacturers include the construction of a base in their service; others leave this to the customer.

Most brochures mention rainwater gutters and downpipes as optional extras, but as far as most local authorities are concerned, there is very little option. The necessary rainwater goods can cost as much as 10 per cent extra on the cost of the basic garage and, in addition, disposal of the rainwater (for example, drains leading to a soakaway) must be provided.

Nearly all garages, particularly those made of concrete, are offered with a choice of main doors. Personal side doors, special wall panels containing either fixed or opening windows, and other items are usually optional, at extra cost.

ground floor extensions

Some of the prefabricated structures which manufacturers claim to be home extensions cannot be used as living accommodation, because they do not comply with all the numerous requirements of the Building Regulations for a habitable room. The basic requirements for a habitable room are that it must have a ceiling height of at least 2·3 metres (about 7 feet 7 inches), and its walls and roof must have the required degrees of thermal insulation and fire resistance. For instance, translucent roofs (pvc, glass fibre, glass) do not on their own provide the degree of thermal insulation required for a habitable room (but some manufacturers' literature shows pictures of translucent-roofed rooms being used as living rooms). Solid flat roofs constructed of asbestos-cement sheeting with polystyrene bonded to it provide sufficient thermal insulation. Most manufacturers can provide the prescribed degree of thermal insulation in prefabricated wall panels, but these are likely to cost more than standard panels.

Special panels which meet the requirements for fire resistance are also usually more expensive than standard wall panels.

In the case of a room which is to be used as a habitable room, the floor must be protected from damp penetration. Unless the manufacturer undertakes to construct the foundations or base necessary for a habitable room, the price a builder would charge for this work must be added to the total cost.

A report in *Handyman Which?* May 1973 included prefabricated extensions.

First, the ground is prepared by clearing and levelling it. If the site is damp, it may be necessary to have new land drains installed. These are perforated or porous pipes which are laid just under the surface of the ground at a gradient to drain moisture away to an open drain or a soakaway. If existing land drains are damaged when the site is being prepared, they must be repaired or replaced.

drains

If an existing drain runs under the site of the proposed extension, it must be protected so that it cannot be damaged by the additional loads which are likely to be placed over it. If the drain consists of stoneware pipes, they may have to be surrounded by up to 6 inches (about 150 mm) of concrete. If a stoneware drain is not very deep or is in poor condition, it is safer to have it replaced with a cast iron one. Similarly, where the run-in for a new garage is over a drain, precautions may have to be taken to avoid damage to the pipes.

When new drains are laid, they too have to be adequately protected against possible damage. The local authority building control officer arranges for them to be tested for airtightness and watertightness, and to check that they are suitably protected before they are covered up.

New underground drains are made of stoneware or pitch fibre or pvc pipes. Pitch fibre and pvc are cheaper and easier to handle but may not be allowed for soil pipes.

An existing inspection chamber can be left inside a new building provided it is fitted with an airtight cover fixed down with screws or bolts so that it can be removed if the drain has to be inspected. However, a building inspector usually requires an inspection chamber in such a position to be closed up and replaced by a new one outside the new building. If there is an open gully in the area to be built over, it should either be replaced with a back inlet type of gully with a screwed down cover, or be moved to outside the new building.

foundations

The foundations of the walls must be put deep enough into the ground for the weight of the wall and any load which it carries to have a firm base.

The size and depth of foundations depend mainly on the load to be supported and the bearing pressure of the ground (the load per square foot it can take without any risk of subsidence). In most cases it is necessary to provide proper foundations for the new structure at the same depth as the existing building.

The most common type of foundation for external walls is a concrete strip foundation. A hole is dug about a metre deep and concrete poured in to make a strip not less than 150 mm thick, projecting about 150 mm beyond each side of the wall it will support. It is left for a couple of days to set.

Internal walls which support only their own weight, and other walls which support only small loads—not the roof, for instance—can, unless the subsoil is very bad, be built on to the concrete laid down for the floor, provided that the concrete is made extra thick underneath a wall to support its weight.

WALL FOUNDATIONS

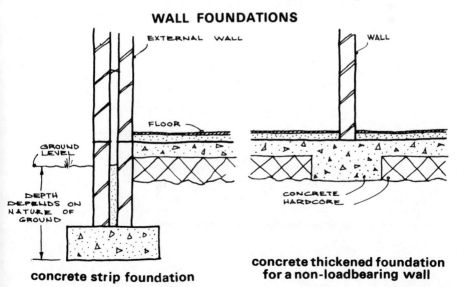

concrete strip foundation

concrete thickened foundation for a non-loadbearing wall

When the foundations are set, the walls are brought up to the level of the damp-proof course (in every external wall, a damp-proof course must be built in at least 6 inches (about 150 mm) above the finished surface of the adjoining ground) and then left while the base of the floor is being constructed.

To prepare for the floor, first, the topsoil is removed. The ground is then covered with a layer of hardcore—solid material such as clean clinker or broken brick. The hardcore must not contain any vegetation, or other matter which could settle or in any way subsequently damage the floor above. Then the hardcore is covered with a layer of concrete.

floor construction

No more work is done on a solid floor construction until the roof is on. But if the extension is having a suspended floor, some more of the construction work is done at this stage.

A suspended timber floor is supported by joists, usually resting on intermediate brick supports, known as sleeper walls. The sleeper walls are either built on to the layer of concrete (the oversite) which is thickened to support them, or go through it to a concrete strip foundation below. The sleeper walls are of honey-

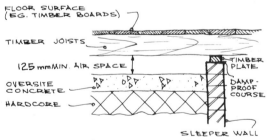

suspended floor construction

comb construction, with a space between each brick to maintain ventilation. (If the joists have to span only a relatively short distance, sleeper walls may not be needed. The joists can be built into the side walls so that the ends are adequately supported by the brickwork of the walls.)

The top of the concrete under the floor must not be lower than the highest level of the ground outside or of any paving adjoining an external wall. Otherwise, there is the risk that dampness or water may come through the wall and gather on top of the concrete oversite in the gap beneath the floor.

Normally, tongued and grooved boards, or other similar inter-locking floor surfaces, form an adequate barrier to prevent any dampness rising from the subsoil into the room above. If the site is very damp, a damp-proof membrane may have to be incorporated in the oversite concrete as an additional precaution.

To ensure adequate ventilation underneath a suspended timber floor, air bricks must be put in the external walls below floor level. If the existing building has a suspended timber floor, there will already be air bricks in one or more of the external walls. It may be possible to use them as part of the ventilation to the new flooring, too.

If constructing a solid floor for the new part when the existing building has a suspended floor, care must be taken that air bricks in the external wall of the existing building do not get blocked up. If there is no possibility of repositioning them in other external walls, as often occurs where a terraced house is being extended across its entire width, the solution is to build air ducts to connect the air bricks in the existing wall to air bricks built into the new external wall.

On no account should a suspended timber floor be left without sufficient air bricks to provide ventilation, otherwise dry rot can develop. It is a good idea, therefore, to have the underfloor ventilation to the rest of your house checked by the builder while he is working on the site, to make sure that no existing air bricks anywhere have become blocked or covered.

external walls

The damp-proof course which is built into the external walls is usually a continuous strip of bituminous felt. If the floor is to be of solid construction, the damp-proof course will be joined with the damp-proof membrane to form a continuous layer.

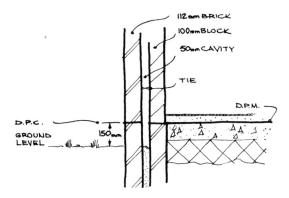

joining damp-proof course and damp-proof membrane

If the level of the floor surface inside is lower than 6 inches (about 150 mm) above the ground level outside, the damp-proof course has to go vertically from the inner leaf of the cavity wall to join with the damp-proof membrane in the floor. If the vertical damp-proofing is on the room side of the inner wall and is plastered over, care must be taken not to pierce it when nailing any skirting to the wall. Where it is possible to lower the ground level outside sufficiently, stepping-down the damp-proof course can be avoided.

The external walls are made of bricks or concrete blocks. The bricks in existing external walls are $4\frac{1}{2}$ inches wide; equivalent bricks made now to metric standards are 112·5 mm wide. Aerated concrete or lightweight concrete blocks come in various widths up to 225 mm (about 9 inches), and so do hollow concrete blocks. *Handyman Which?* reported on bricks and blocks in August 1975.

Breeze blocks are generally suitable only for internal walls, and should not be used for external walls unless rendered. If concrete blocks are specified, make sure the builder does not instead use breeze blocks as a cheap substitute. Concrete blocks are pale grey usually and tend to be powdery to the touch, whereas breeze blocks are a dark bluish grey and are made of what looks like the clinker one would get in the grate after burning a lot of coal or coke.

Where new bricks or blocks join on to an existing wall they must be properly integrated. This can be done by either block-bonding or toothing. Toothing is visually neater but is more expensive. If you have specified toothing, watch that the builder does not do the

existing wall   **new wall block-bonded into existing wall**   **new wall toothed into existing wall**

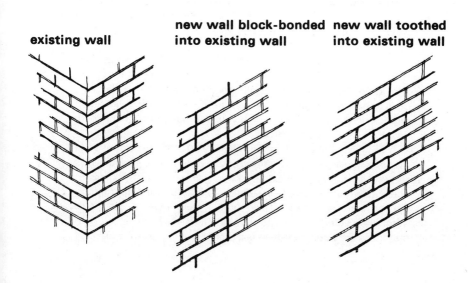

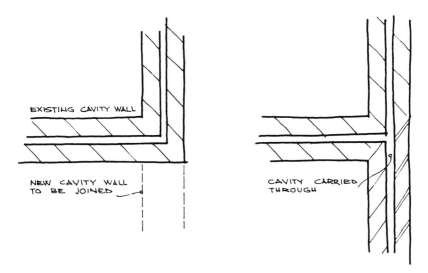

cheaper block-bonding instead. If you cannot get new bricks to match the old in size, block-bonding may have to be adopted.

When a new cavity wall is being joined to an existing cavity wall, the cavity should be carried through by removing part of one of the existing leaves at the junction. Each leaf of a cavity wall should be at least 100 mm thick; in some circumstances the inner leaf can be 75 mm. Both leaves of the cavity wall are made of bricks up to the level of the damp-proof course; above that, the inner leaf can be lightweight concrete blocks.

The width of the cavity between the two leaves must be not less than 50 mm nor more than 75 mm. It is important that the cavity should not be closed at any point through the builder's careless-ness or bad workmanship, letting bits of mortar or rubbish fall in during construction of the wall. If you find that this has happened, get the builder to clear it out.

A solid external wall must be at least 200 mm if the extension is part of a house. A typical method of construction for a solid wall is to bond two lines of bricks together, giving a total thickness of about 225 mm. Alternatively, concrete blocks of the appropriate thickness are used. If the building is a greenhouse or a store or other outbuilding under 3 metres high, the walls need be only 100 mm thick, provided that there is a pier at least 200 mm square, at least every 3 metres, and that the mortar used is of specified strength and that the roof is so designed as not to push the walls outwards.

doors and windows

As the walls go up, door and window frames are built in.

Mass-produced doors and windows, both timber framed and metal framed, are available in a wide range of patterns and sizes. The cost of a ready-made unit is much less than an equivalent made-to-measure unit, so if the door and window openings are designed to standard sizes, the costs are kept down. The sizes quoted in manufacturers' literature for window units are the overall dimensions; for doors, the sizes do not include the frames.

The frames are available made in softwood, hardwood (which is more attractive, but more expensive), plastic-coated timber (expensive but relatively maintenance-free), galvanised mild steel, aluminium with a natural finish, or anodised aluminium with a surface coating which is more corrosion-resistant and decorative, but costs more.

If you want to have double glazing, the builder or your architect, building surveyor or architectural consultant can tell you about the various types that might be suitable. If you decide to fit the type of unit that consists of two panes of glass bonded together at the edges and an air space between, and the window frames are not deep enough to take the double panes, it is possible to use a 'stepped' unit in which the inner pane is smaller and fits just inside the frame. A report on double glazing in *Handyman Which?* November 1973 was updated in August 1975.

A builder usually puts a timber window ledge on the inside of the windows. If you want a ledge of any different material, such as quarry tiles or ceramic tiles, tell the builder before he starts.

Roof

As soon as the walls are high enough, the roof is constructed and the covering put on.

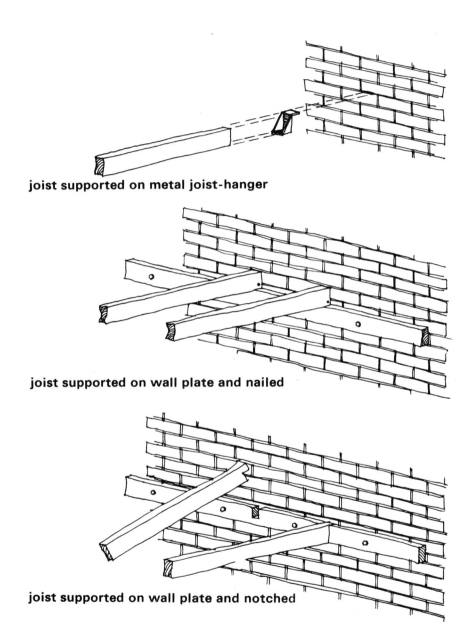

joist supported on metal joist-hanger

joist supported on wall plate and nailed

joist supported on wall plate and notched

flat roof

If the joists of a new flat roof span on to an existing wall, there are three alternative methods of providing support: to form holes in the existing wall and build in each new joist, to bolt a piece of timber (a wall plate) on to the existing wall and nail or notch each new joist into it, or to fix metal hanging brackets into the existing wall and rest each new joist into one.

The deck of a flat roof is tilted either by tapering the joists along their top edge where they support the deck or, more commonly, by fixing long thin wedges, known as firring pieces, to the top of the joists. The least amount of fall of a flat roof is usually 1 in 60 (or 5 mm for every 300 mm). The white or light grey mineral chippings embedded in the top layer of roofing felt give the roof additional fire resistance and reflect the heat of the sun. The fascia board on which the gutter is fixed can be either flush against the wall or, if the roof has overhanging eaves, fixed across the ends of the projecting joists. The under-side of such joists is sealed with what is known as a soffit board.

flat roof construction

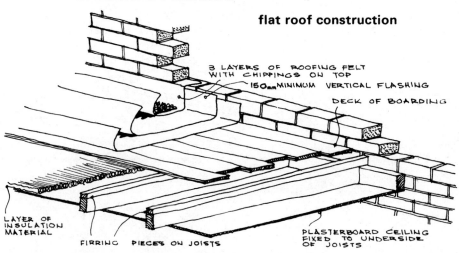

3 LAYERS OF ROOFING FELT WITH CHIPPINGS ON TOP

150mm MINIMUM VERTICAL FLASHING

DECK OF BOARDING

LAYER OF INSULATION MATERIAL

FIRRING PIECES ON JOISTS

PLASTERBOARD CEILING FIXED TO UNDERSIDE OF JOISTS

To ensure that the roof remains watertight and gets rid of the rainwater which falls on it, the roof covering must be sealed (by what is known as flashing) at any vertical surfaces it rests against—the outside wall of the existing building, for example. Flashing must extend to a height of at least 150 mm (about 6 inches) above the surface of the new roof so that rainwater does not penetrate at the angle with the vertical surface. In many cases, the roof covering itself can act as the flashing by being continued up the vertical wall.

pitched roof

Rafters, joined with ceiling joists to form triangles, are connected at the lower corners by a piece of timber (the wall plate) on top of the wall to which the joists are fixed, and at the apex by a piece of

pitched roof construction

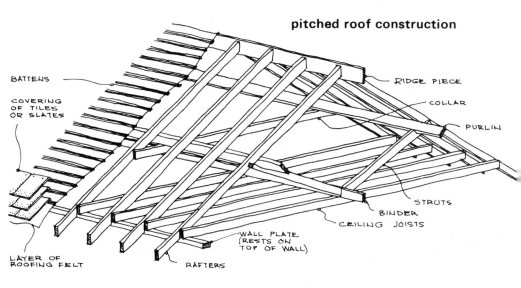

BATTENS

COVERING OF TILES OR SLATES

RIDGE PIECE

COLLAR

PURLIN

STRUTS

BINDER

CEILING JOISTS

WALL PLATE (RESTS ON TOP OF WALL)

LAYER OF ROOFING FELT

RAFTERS

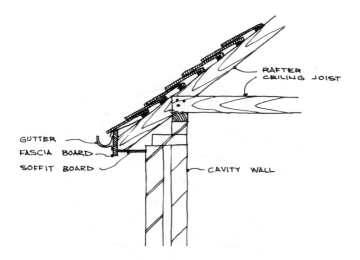

timber known as the ridge piece. If the rafters are particularly long, because the roof is high, they are prevented from sagging by additional support, usually half-way up each rafter, in the form of horizontal timber beams known as purlins. Long ceiling joists are prevented from distorting by timber binders running at right angles across the top of the joists, holding them together. Purlins can be given support by timber struts, which are sometimes braced (by what is called the collar) where they meet the purlins. A reinforced roofing felt is usually fixed over the rafters before putting on the battens; to ensure a completely weatherproof covering, this should extend right down to the gutter. Slates are nailed on to timber battens which are fixed to the rafters. Tiles are moulded with nibs or projections at the top edge which lodge on the battens, and usually only every fourth row is nailed.

Fascia and soffit boards are fixed to the lower ends of the rafters, and the gutter attached to the fascia board. On a pitched roof with a gable end, it is common for the horizontal roof timbers to be continued beyond the end wall, with the roof covering going several inches over the end of the wall to form a projecting verge. Boards called barge boards are put on as facing to the outer edge of the verge, and soffit boards are added to fill in the underside.

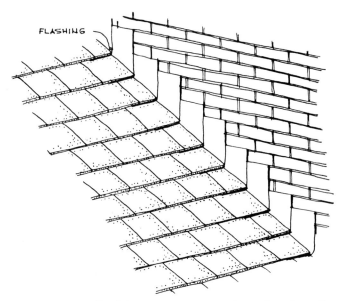

FLASHING

flashing at junction of roof and wall

At the junction of a pitched roof or a lean-to roof and an existing wall, flashing is necessary so that there is no gap through which rainwater can penetrate.

treatment of roof timbers

In certain areas of the country, predominantly in the south, soft-wood timber used in any part of the construction of a roof must be treated with a preservative to prevent infestation by the house longhorn beetle, which is active in those areas. Where applicable, builders buy timber already treated. You will notice that treated timber has a greenish or dark brown colour.

ceiling

The ceiling is put on later. It is fixed to the joists forming part of the roof construction (pitched or flat). Ceilings are usually plaster-board, sometimes with a plaster coating. Timber boarding or other sheet materials can be used, provided they conform to the fire precaution regulations. Above the ceiling there has to be an insulating layer. With a solid flat roof, a deck constructed of 50 mm (about 2 inches) thick wood-wool slabs bonded to 32 mm (about $1\frac{1}{4}$ inches) thick polystyrene, or a deck of timber boarding with at least 75 mm (about 3 inches) glass fibre underneath, would satisfy the insulation requirements. With a pitched roof, a 75 mm thick layer of glass fibre above the ceiling, or about the same thickness of vermiculite loose-fill would provide adequate insulation. *Handyman Which?* August 1975 was about insulation.

translucent roof

Pvc and translucent glass fibre roofing is manufactured in sheets of various sizes, usually with a corrugated or similarly ridged profile. The sheets can be interlocked to make the finished surface completely watertight. The longitudinal overlap depends on the angle at which the roof slopes: the shallower the angle, the greater the risk of capillary action between overlapping sheets, so the longer the overlap. Since these sheets are virtually self-supporting in the direction of their corrugation, rafters are not necessary for them; generally only purlins are needed as support.

If the covering is wired glass, this is supported between bars, timber or metal, which perform the same function as rafters. Aluminium bars are often used; although a little more expensive, they do not need much subsequent maintenance in the way of painting.

As with any lean-to roof, flashing is necessary at the junction with the existing wall. Some manufacturers of corrugated sheeting provide prefabricated flashing of the same profile and material as the sheeting, shaped to be built into an existing wall.

gutter on flat roof (cross-section)

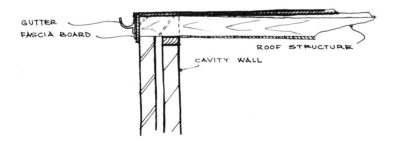

GUTTER
FASCIA BOARD
ROOF STRUCTURE
CAVITY WALL

gutter on flat roof with projecting eaves (cross-section)

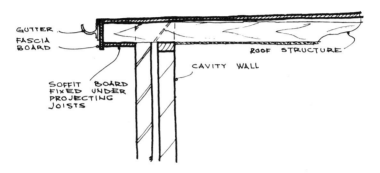

GUTTER
FASCIA
BOARD
ROOF STRUCTURE
CAVITY WALL
SOFFIT BOARD
FIXED UNDER
PROJECTING
JOISTS

gutter behind parapet wall (cross-section)

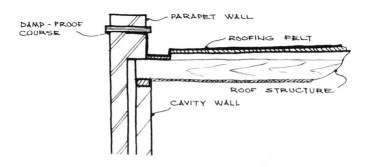

DAMP-PROOF
COURSE
PARAPET WALL
ROOFING FELT
ROOF STRUCTURE
CAVITY WALL

rainwater pipes

A gutter consists of several individual lengths of guttering, and is fixed at a slight slope, allowing all rainwater falling into it to flow away.

At one time, rainwater goods were made only of cast iron, but asbestos cement has been used, and now pvc is common because it is inexpensive and requires virtually no maintenance.

A gutter is fixed to the fascia board by brackets. The gutter slopes slightly to the vertical rainwater pipe, which is connected to it with a special fitting. An internal rainwater pipe from a gutter in a parapet is encased in a duct, generally with removable panels so that the pipe can be cleaned or replaced when necessary. The duct projects about 150 mm (about 6 inches) from the inside walls all the way down. The gutter in the parapet is usually lined with lead or roofing felt, which has to be flashed up against the inside of the parapet wall. The gutter can slope to one corner and there discharge into a vertical pipe. Alternatively, the gutter can slope from both ends towards a central position behind the parapet wall, and discharge either through the wall into a vertical pipe on the face of the wall or out of sight down a pipe built in behind the wall.

The open end at the top of any vertical pipe should have a wire or plastic cage put over it. This is referred to as a balloon. It prevents rubbish, falling leaves or birds' nests from blocking the pipe. Builders sometimes forget about fitting a cage, so make sure one is put on.

Internal work

Once the roof is up and the windows glazed, the internal work can be completed, starting with the floor.

solid floors

If you are having a solid floor construction, a damp-proof membrane is applied on top of the concrete to prevent any damp from rising into the building. The damp-proof layers in the new and the existing structures should be integrated so that there is no chance of damp creeping in at the joins. It is preferable for the new damp-proof membrane to be at the same level as the existing one, but if a difference in levels cannot be avoided, the damp-proofing can be joined by forming a step at the junction.

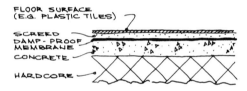

solid floor construction

The nature of the damp-proof membrane depends on the final floor surface you are having. For a covering of cork or plastic, the damp-proof membrane has to be covered with an inch or two of screed (a mix of sand and cement) to ensure a level enough surface. If the floor surface is to be timber boards, battens are embedded in the screed, for the boards to be fixed to them. The battens should be impregnated against rot, and possibly the boarding, too.

suspended floors

The sleeper walls have to have a damp-proof course to prevent damp from rising to the floor timbers through the bricks. Above each sleeper wall a length of timber is laid (called a plate) to which the joists are nailed. There must be a space of at least 125 mm (5 inches) between the top of the oversite and the joist suspended over it. This space must be clear of all debris to allow free passage of air. Some workmen tend to use this space as a rubbish dump, so you should keep an eye on them, or ask the builder to do so, to make sure that it is left clear and free from sawdust and shavings before the boards are laid.

The top surface of the floor can be boards or sheets of wood chipboard. If the final covering is to be a semi-rigid one, such as plastic tiles or sheeting or cork tiles, a protective layer of hardboard must be put on top of boards to prevent differential movement. Carpets do not need the protection of hardboard because the underfelt provides much the same barrier.

The floor of an upper storey is always of suspended construction, with the joists supported by the brickwork of the walls. The joists are put in as the walls go up. Floor boards or other surface coverings are laid after the roof is on.

inside walls

Internal wall surfaces are generally plastered because plaster gives the most versatile finish. An alternative to plastering brick walls is to attach timber boarding to battens fixed across the walls. Fire precaution requirements restrict the use of surface materials which allow flame to spread. Untreated timber boarding can be used on walls only if the total area does not exceed half the floor area of the room, up to a maximum boarded area of 20 square metres (about 215 square feet). If timber boarding treated with a flame-retardant liquid is used, or a wall board made with a top layer of material classified as having a very low flame spread, there is no restriction on the boarded area.

A timber frame wall consists of vertical and horizontal pieces of timber, about 75 mm or 100 mm (3 or 4 inches) across, fixed together with the vertical pieces of timber spaced about 450 mm (about 1 foot 6 inches) apart and the horizontal pieces about 1200 mm (about 4 feet) apart. A covering of some type of boarding, often plasterboard, is then fixed to each side of the timber frame, leaving a space the width of the timber pieces between. If the plasterboard on timber frame walls is primed, it can be wallpapered without further treatment. If it is to be painted, it is preferable first to apply a thin coat of plaster over the board to give a smooth surface. An inherent disadvantage of timber frame walls is that the plasterboard area does not provide adequate support for pictures or shelves or any other heavy object which you may want to hang on the inside wall; you can only safely put fixing nails where the timber pieces are.

timber frame (studding) wall construction

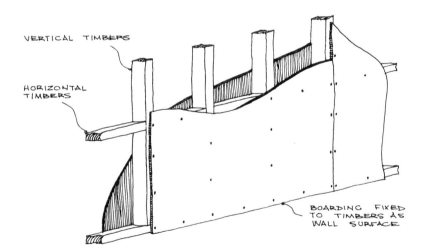

VERTICAL TIMBERS

HORIZONTAL TIMBERS

BOARDING FIXED TO TIMBERS AS WALL SURFACE

existing walls

An existing wall must not be demolished without retaining or putting in a sufficiently strong beam or joist to provide the necessary support.

An extension nearly always turns an existing external wall into an internal wall, and this needs to be finished and decorated in the same way as the inside surfaces of the new walls. An external wall, particularly a north-facing one, may have collected green algae, and these must be killed by the application of a suitable fungicide and brushed off, otherwise the algae may stain any subsequent decorations, even through plaster.

Some bricks used for external walls collect chemical salts on their outer surface, derived either from the bricks themselves or from the mortar. These salts should be brushed off at frequent intervals during construction. In severe cases, the subsequent decoration of such a wall may have to be delayed for some months because paper or gloss paint would be blistered and damaged by the salts. So, until the efflorescence dies down, a permeable and cheap wall finish, such as distemper, should be applied. An expensive but certain remedy is to line severely affected walls with a bituminous corrugated sheet before plastering, or to fix preservative-impregnated battens and a plasterboard lining.

pipes

All new pipes leading from soil and waste appliances must be watertight and airtight, and there must be sufficient fall in all pipes to ensure that the effluent flows away properly. Each appliance must be equipped with a water-sealed trap, in the form of a double bend in the outlet pipe, to prevent odours in the drains from reaching the appliance. It must be possible to clean out every trap and length of pipe, and therefore a threaded plug, called a cleaning eye, has to be incorporated at each bend in a pipe and at every trap above the ground.

Lavatories are manufactured with an integral water-sealed trap and a 4-inch (100 mm) diameter outlet to be connected direct to a

E

new soil pipe or drain. A waste appliance such as a wash basin, however, is not usually manufactured with a trap, and a trap has to be bought separately and fitted to the outlet of the appliance.

In a house built before the Building Regulations came into force (February 1966), or one of not more than three storeys, soil and waste pipes can be put inside or outside the building (but no waste water pipe is allowed to discharge into a hopper head). In all other cases, the pipes must be put inside.

A waste pipe from an appliance at ground floor level connects to the drain outside usually by means of a gully. Whereas a rainwater pipe is allowed to discharge over the grating of a gully, a waste pipe must discharge below the level of the grating, and above the water level in the trap of the gully. A back inlet type of gully is commonly used because it not only complies with the regulations but also has a tidy appearance.

A drain serving a soil appliance must always connect in a straight line to an inspection chamber, but the drain from a gully

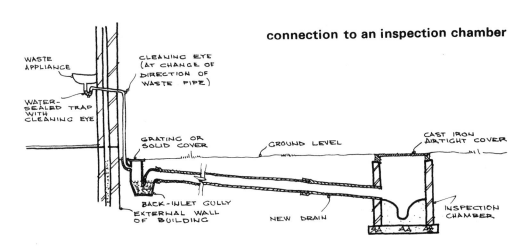

connection to an inspection chamber

WASTE APPLIANCE

CLEANING EYE (AT CHANGE OF DIRECTION OF WASTE PIPE)

WATER-SEALED TRAP WITH CLEANING EYE

GRATING OR SOLID COVER

GROUND LEVEL

CAST IRON AIRTIGHT COVER

BACK-INLET GULLY
EXTERNAL WALL OF BUILDING

NEW DRAIN

INSPECTION CHAMBER

collecting waste water from a bathroom only may in some cases be joined to another drain which has adequate access for cleaning, without an inspection chamber at the junction.

A new first-floor bathroom with a lavatory necessitates a new soil and vent pipe connecting to the underground drains, unless there is one near enough for a new connection to be made easily to it. If the house was built before the introduction of the Building Regulations, the local authority may permit a new soil and vent pipe to be put outside the building; otherwise the pipe has to run up through the house.

The positions for the hot and cold water pipes are not usually shown on the drawings for an extension scheme. Generally, the plumber who carries out the work installs the various pipes and pipe-fittings in the positions he thinks best and most convenient. If you want the pipe work to be concealed, or as unobtrusive as possible, you should discuss this with the plumber beforehand.

A flue pipe from a gas appliance must be enclosed in a sleeve of non-combustible material where it passes through any roof, floor, ceiling, wall or partition made of combustible material, or where anyone might lean against it or touch it and get burnt. The pipe does not have to have a sleeve where it passes through an enclosed space to which one has access, such as a cupboard or duct or a roof area.

electrical work

Most extensions necessitate a certain amount of electrical work, even if only the provision of an additional lighting point or two. Drawings and specifications seldom show the precise extent of this work: you have to tell the builder either to include in his price for so-many new socket outlets and so-many new lighting points, or to include a PC sum for electrical work in the total price he quotes you.

Where the installation is straightforward, electrical work may be priced at so-much per socket outlet and so-much per lighting point. This includes the necessary sockets, wiring and switches, but not lighting fittings, which you can choose later and buy separately from another source.

The electrician has to be told how many points you want, and where they should be. They are fairly expensive, but generally it is better to have one or two extra points, rather than too few. The electrician may tell you that you must have a new ring circuit installed. And if the existing wiring is rather old, this might be an opportunity to have the whole house re-wired. If a new connection to the meter itself is required, you will have to arrange with the electricity board for this to be done. In any case, you should notify them that you are having an extension made to your electrical installation. The board may want to inspect the new installation before connecting the supply.

If the existing central heating system cannot take any more radiators to heat the extension and you consider installing off-peak electric storage heaters there, now is the time to have the wiring put in, even if you do not intend to put them in until some time later.

Variations

During the course of the work you may have to agree to variations owing to unforeseen circumstances, or you may change your mind about some aspect. Any change of mind is likely to cost money. The builder will accept your altered instructions but may not warn you of the expense involved. Therefore, ask what any change will cost before agreeing the variation with the builder, even if only an extra electric socket or tiling a bathroom wall. With some variations, a corresponding deduction should be shown in the amended price: for example, an additional window means a saving in brickwork. All variations must be confirmed in writing and signed by both parties.

A major variation may need fresh application to the local authority for approval.

The work should be finished within the period stated in the contract. If not, you can invoke the clause in the contract whereby the builder has to pay you a specified amount for any expenses you incur for every week or part of a week he falls behind the completion date. Sometimes a builder asks for an extension of the time originally estimated because of circumstances arising since the work started. It is up to you whether you agree to this variation.

If you had an architect, building surveyor or architectural consultant supervising the work, the builder will submit his accounts to him, and he should arrange for any defects to be made good. When he is satisfied with the work, he issues to the builder a certificate stating that the account is in order. It is this certificate which the builder presents to you for payment. In this way it is the architect's, surveyor's or consultant's responsibility that the work charged for is satisfactory. If it is not, you cannot claim against the builder—but you can claim against the architect, building surveyor or architectural consultant.

If you did not have a professional supervisor, the builder will submit his account to you. It should indicate the original contract price (less any interim payments which you may have made by agreement) plus or minus any sums agreed as variations to the contract. Pay particular attention to the charges for any addition to the work specified in the original contract, and any adjustments that should be made for provisional sums. If any work previously specified was omitted by agreement, the appropriate deduction should appear.

The builder should show you receipted accounts for PC items, not just invoices. These may show the retail price less trade discount; you should be prepared to pay the builder about 5 per cent more than the trade price he paid. If you had already paid for any fittings listed under the PC items (wallpaper, for instance, or a gas heater), these amounts should not be included in his bill.

Make sure that all the work has been completed to your satisfaction. If you consider that any part of the work is not finished, inform the builder in writing and request him to finish the work and re-submit his account, dated accordingly.

The local authority building control office has to be notified when the builder has completed the work so that the final inspection can be made. If the building control officer finds any work is not in accordance with the Building Regulations, he will require the contravention to be remedied. Unless you were present when the building control officer made his inspection, it is worth finding out from his office, when you get the builder's account, whether the final inspection has been made and whether the work was considered satisfactory. However, the building control officer will have inspected the finished work only to check that it complies with the Building Regulations, and he is not concerned with every aspect of the work: decorations or standards of craftmanship or finish, for example, are of no interest to him. So you should make a thorough inspection yourself to find out whether all your requirements have been met. It is relatively easy to check for more superficial defects such as floors not level, uneven plaster, badly-fitting doors, poor decoration. Any defects should be listed, and the list handed to the builder with a covering letter, where possible referring to the appropriate clause in the contract. A generally poor standard of work is often difficult to define as a defect, but would count as 'work not being done in a good and workmanlike manner'. Any defective or unfinished work should be made good by the builder within the time specified in the contract.

The account should then be paid, with the exception of any percentage which it was agreed should be retained for the specified period, usually three to six months. You should make a further inspection towards the end of this liability period—say, two weeks before its expiration—to make sure all is well before paying the final amount.

Insurance

If the value of the house has increased as a result of the extension, as is likely to be the case, you should increase your insurance for the house accordingly, when the work has been completed.

Rates

Any substantial improvement to property is likely to increase the rates on it, or to be more precise, to put up its rateable value.

The local rating authority fixes the rate in the pound to be paid on property in its area, sends out rate demands, and collects the money. It does not itself decide the rateable value of a property. The Inland Revenue's local valuation officer is the person who assesses or re-assesses rateable values. He can require a house-holder to give him any information needed to keep the rateable value of a property correct, and he has the right to come and inspect the property. It is the responsibility of a local authority —not the owner—to notify the valuation officer when it knows of any improvement to a property which may have increased the value of the property. The local authority's main source of information is the building control office's register of notifications and approvals.

If a property is altered, an inspection is made by the valuation officer or his representative. If the valuation officer then considers that the alteration has affected the hypothetical annual rental value on which the rateable value is based, he sends to the occupier a form which states that he proposes to alter the existing entry in the valuation list. The existing and proposed entries are indicated, and the back of the form tells how one can object to the proposal.

If no objection is made to the re-assessed rateable value within the time specified in the notice, this new value will be attributed to the property, and subsequent demands issued by the rating authority will be based on this figure.

The increase in the amount which you actually have to pay depends on the current rate per pound for the area. The latter figure is never affected by any alterations made to property.

METRIC CONVERSIONS

Area

metric measurement	approximate imperial equivalent	imperial measurement	metric equivalent
10 000 mm²	$15\frac{1}{2}$ sq in	1 sq in	0.006 m²
100 000 mm² (0.1 m²)	155 sq in	144 sq in (1 sq ft)	0.093 m²
		9 sq ft (1 sq yd)	0.836 m²
m²	**sq ft**	1 acre (4,840 sq yd)	0.405 ha
1	$10\frac{3}{4}$		
2	$21\frac{1}{2}$		
3	$32\frac{1}{4}$		
4	43		
6	$64\frac{1}{2}$		
10	$107\frac{1}{2}$		
15	$161\frac{1}{2}$		
20	$215\frac{1}{4}$		
30	323		
40	$430\frac{1}{2}$		
10 000 = 1 hectare (ha)	just under $2\frac{1}{2}$ acres		

Volume

imperial measurement	metric equivalent
cu ft	**m³**
1	0.028
10	0.283
100	2.831
500	14.158
1,000	28.316
1,500	42.474
1,750	49.554
2,000	56.632
4,000	113.264

Length

metric measurement	approximate imperial equivalent		imperial measurement		metric equivalent
mm	**ft**	**in**	**ft**	**in**	**mm**
10 (1 cm)		$\frac{3}{8}$		$\frac{3}{8}$	9.5
12		$\frac{1}{2}$		$\frac{1}{2}$	12.7
16		$\frac{5}{8}$		$\frac{5}{8}$	15.9
20		$\frac{3}{4}$		1	25.4
25		1		$1\frac{1}{2}$	38·1
50		2		2	50.8
75		3		3	76.2
100		4		4	101.6
112		$4\frac{1}{2}$		5	127.0
150		$5\frac{7}{8}$		6	152.4
200		$7\frac{7}{8}$		7	177.8
220		$8\frac{5}{8}$		8	203.2
300		$11\frac{3}{4}$		9	228.6
400	1	$3\frac{3}{4}$		10	254.0
500 (0·5 m)	1	$6\frac{3}{4}$		11	279.4
600	1	$11\frac{5}{8}$	1	0	304.8
700	2	$3\frac{5}{8}$	1	6	457.2
800	2	$7\frac{1}{2}$	2	0	609.6
900	2	$11\frac{3}{8}$	2	6	762.0
1 000 (1 m)	3	$3\frac{3}{8}$	3	0 (1 yd)	914.4
m					**m**
1	3	$3\frac{3}{8}$	3	6	1.066
1.2	3	$11\frac{1}{4}$	4	0	1.219
1.5	4	11	5	0	1.524
2	6	$6\frac{3}{4}$	6	0	1.828
2.3	7	7	7	0	2.133
2.5	8	$2\frac{3}{8}$	7	6	2.286
3	9	$10\frac{1}{8}$	8	0	2.438
3.5	11	7	9	0	2.743
4	13	$1\frac{1}{2}$	10	0	3.048
5	16	$4\frac{1}{2}$	11	0	3.352
6	19	$8\frac{1}{4}$	12	0	3.657
7	22	$11\frac{5}{8}$			
8	26	3			
9	29	6			
10	32	$10\frac{1}{8}$			
25	82	$0\frac{1}{4}$			

OUTLINE PROGRAMME FOR AN EXTENSION

formulate ideas

put ideas on paper, as a sketch

decide on what professional advice to have, and at what stages (you can engage an architect, building surveyor or architectural consultant to undertake any, some or all of the following operations)

obtain estimates of likely cost, from builders

get drawings and specification produced

obtain necessary approvals

prepare contract

obtain quotations (tenders) from several builders

appoint builder: complete and sign contract

supervise construction

check accounts submitted

pay builder's final account
(less 5 per cent of contract sum)

inspect work for possible defects

pay balance to builder

air brick	a brick with holes through it, used for ventilating larders, lavatories, spaces under suspended floors
back-inlet gully (b.i.g.) (b.i.t.g.)	gully which has an integral socket in its side so that pipes connect to the socket and do not discharge water into the top of the gully

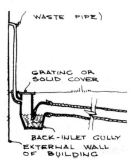

balanced flue	a special kind of duct connecting a gas appliance direct to the external air: one part conveys fresh air to the appliance and the other part conveys the fumes from the appliance out to the external air
balloon	a cage fitting over the open end at the top of a vertical pipe
barge boards	timber boards fixed to a gable end of a roof along the exposed edge of the tiles

battens

long, thin pieces of timber used in roof construction; tiles or slates are fixed to battens

bearing pressure

in relation to subsoil, the pressure which subsoil can bear safely before it starts to compress

bill of quantities

a document prepared by a quantity surveyor to enable a builder to estimate the cost of a building or other work as shown on the drawings and described in the specification prepared by an architect; consists of items which give in detail the quantities and descriptions of the various materials and labour required

binder

in roof construction, a beam (usually timber) running at right angles to ceiling joists and fixed to the top of the joists in order to bind them all together

block-bonding

a method of joining two walls together, usually only when a new wall is being joined to an existing one

block plan

plan showing the proposed work in relation to the site

breeze blocks

blocks made of a mixture of cement and ash aggregate, used instead of bricks for building walls

building line   an imaginary line on either side of a road or street in front of which no building is allowed

built-up roofing   two or more layers of bitumen-based roofing felt

cavity wall   a wall built as two separate halves with an air space between, linked together with metal ties

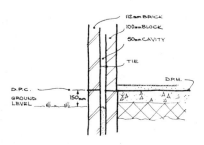

cladding   wall covering, especially one provided externally for weather protection

cleaning eye   a small orifice in a waste pipe, fitted with a screw stopper to enable the inside of the pipe to be cleaned out

clinker blocks   blocks made of a mixture of cement and clinker aggregate; similar to breeze blocks

construction notes description of method of construction written on drawings in lieu of a separate specification

cross-section   the view seen if part of an object (or building) were removed; in drawings, the section is usually in a vertical plane

curtilage   the area of land belonging to a particular property (as opposed to a particular person)

damp-proof course (d.p.c.) a continuous layer of waterproof material (e.g. a strip of bituminous felt) built into an external wall as a barrier against damp

damp-proof membrane (d.p.m.) in solid floors, a continuous layer of waterproof material (e.g. heavy-duty polythene sheeting or not less than three coats of a bituminous solution applied by brush) acting as a barrier against rising damp

dormer window a vertical window built into a sloping roof, with its own side walls and roof (either pitched or flat)

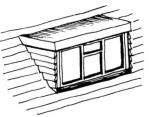

double-seal cover a special kind of cover for inspection chambers: the cover has a double rim as an extra precaution against odours escaping from the drains and is screwed down; usually used where an inspection chamber is under part of a building

drain pipe below ground, part of a drainage system; can be made of pitch fibre, pvc, stoneware (s.g.w.) or cast iron

duct a kind of tunnel, made of plywood or sheet metal or other material, for encasing pipes, or for letting air pass through, or for ventilation to an appliance

eaves lower overhanging part of a sloping roof

elevation in drawings, the view of one face of a building (e.g. front elevation)

estimate   approximation of the likely cost of work to
                           be done, before details are available to
                           quote a firm price

fascia board   in roof construction, a long board made of
                           wood fixed vertically around the edges of
                           a roof; gutters are usually fixed to a fascia
                           board

GUTTER
FASCIA BOARD
SOFFIT BOARD

fire resistance   the resistance to fire (expressed as a
                           duration of time) which a material or part
                           of a building is deemed to have, deter-
                           mined by tests in accordance with the
                           appropriate British Standard specifica-
                           tion: a sample is exposed to flame on one
                           side and is timed until it collapses or
                           develops cracks through which flames or
                           hot gases can pass, or gets hotter than a
                           prescribed temperature on the unex-
                           posed side—that length of time is said to
                           be the fire resistance of that particular
                           material or type of construction

firring pieces   in a solid flat roof construction, long
                           pieces of timber fixed to the top of, and
                           usually the same width as, the joists;
                           thicker one end than the other in order to
                           provide a slight slope for the roof decking

flashing   a continuous strip of waterproof material (e.g. lead or bituminous felt) to prevent the ingress of water where a roof covering abuts a wall

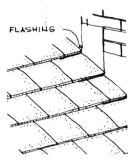

flue   a passage for conveying the discharge of the products of combustion from an appliance to the external air

foul water   water discharged from a house through pipes and drains: waste water, soil water, or both, but not rainwater

glazing bars   bars of timber or metal used to support and join panes of glass roofing

going   in a staircase, the horizontal measurement of the step on which you tread; must be at least 220 mm.

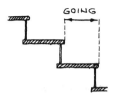

gully	a funnel-shaped receptacle connected to a drain so that pipes discharge into it; the topmost part is at ground level. A gully with an open top is usually fitted with a grating to stop anything solid getting in and causing a blockage
habitable room	a room used for living accommodation, such as a bedroom, living room, sitting room, dining room, study, but not a bathroom nor a hall, scullery or kitchen (unless it is also capable of being used as a breakfast room or dining room)
hanger	in a pitched roof, a vertical piece of timber sometimes put directly under the ridge, connecting it to the joists at two or three points; usually only in older type of construction
hardcore	solid and inert material (e.g. clean clinker or broken bricks) used for forming a firm base on which to lay concrete
hectare (ha)	a unit used in the metric system for measuring large areas of land: 1 hectare is 10 000 square metres (approximately $2\frac{1}{2}$ acres)
hipped roof	a pitched roof where all the sides slope inwards

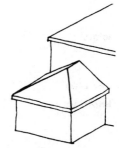

hopper
a box or funnel-shaped receptacle with an outlet, fitted on to a rainwater pipe so that two or more pipes can discharge into it

inspection chamber
a pit with solid walls and a square or round removable cover constructed on a drain to provide access to the drain for inspection and cleaning; also referred to as a manhole

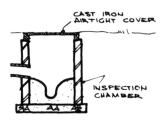

joists
parallel timber members stretching from wall to wall supporting a floor, a flat roof or a ceiling

key plan
location plan

knotting
in relation to decorating, a sealing liquid which is painted over knots in new wood to prevent the resin or turpentine from exuding and affecting the finished surface

lavatory	water closet (w.c.)
lavatory basin	a wash hand basin
leaf	each of the two separate walls comprising a cavity wall
lintol (lintel)	a beam inserted immediately above an opening in a wall (e.g. a window or door opening) in order to support that portion of wall. Lintols can be steel or concrete reinforced with steel rods; older houses may have timber lintols
location plan	a plan showing the position of a house in relation to the surrounding district
manhole	an inspection chamber
metric measurement	international system, based on the unit of a metre (m), now adopted by the building industry in place of the imperial measurements previously used
millimetre (mm)	one thousandth of a metre, the smallest unit of length in the metric system
outline planning permission	permission in principle to carry out a particular development, before giving full details; usually only for large projects
oversite	in relation to a ground floor of the suspended timber type, a layer of concrete which is laid over the whole site, preventing damp from rising out of the ground and affecting the timbers above
partition wall	an internal wall; usually (but not necessarily) non-loadbearing, i.e. supporting no more than its own weight
pier	a column of solid upright masonry or brickwork (square or rectangular in cross-section) which acts as a support either to the structure resting on top or to the wall into which it is built

plasterboard	a lightweight, protective lining material, formed of aerated gypsum backed on both sides with specially prepared paper; manufactured in sheets of various thicknesses, widths and lengths
plate, timber	a piece of timber fixed along or on top of a wall, to which is fixed a timber floor or roof structure, joists or rafters; also referred to as a wall plate
prime cost (PC) sum	in a contract, an approximate price for work or fittings which will eventually be charged at actual cost
primer	in relation to decorating, a special kind of paint which is applied to a raw surface (e.g. new wood) designed to grip the surface in order to provide a stable base for subsequent layers of paint which might otherwise peel off
purlin	in pitched roofs, a horizontal piece of timber fixed to rafters to prevent them from sagging
purpose-built	built to an individual design
quantity surveyor	professional who advises on and controls building costs. One of his functions is to extract from an architect's drawings the quantities of materials and the labour which will be required for a scheme, and to list all these in a bill of quantities (not generally required for a small building project)
quarry tiles	tiles made from clay and used for floor surfacing; such tiles have good wearing properties and are easy to keep clean, but tend to be cold and noisy
quotation	price quoted by builder to carry out work in accordance with contract and drawings and specification

rafters	in a pitched roof, the sloping timbers on which the roof covering rests
rainwater goods	collective term for gutters and rainwater pipes
rainwater pipe (r.w.p.)	a pipe above ground level which conveys rainwater from gutters; also referred to as a downpipe
rendering	layer of cement mix applied to the surface of a wall, either to provide a weather resistant finish to the outer surface of an external wall or as a base coat on internal wall surfaces prior to plastering
ridge piece	in pitched roofs, a long piece of timber at the topmost part of the roof to which the tops of all the rafters are fixed
rise	in a staircase, the height between two consecutive treads; must not be more than 220 mm

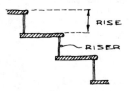

riser	front vertical part of a step
room-sealed appliance	a gas appliance which is designed to operate with a balanced flue; this kind of appliance does not absorb any air from the room in which it is installed
SAA	most stringent grade of fire resistance for a roof construction

screed

in a solid floor construction, a thin layer of a cement and sand mixture, finished with a perfectly smooth surface on to which a flooring material can be directly laid

shoe

integral fitting at the bottom of a down-pipe discharging over a gully. Alternatively, a kind of back inlet gully with no water-sealed trap, fitted to an underground surface water drain so that a rainwater pipe connects directly into it

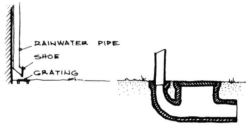

site plan

plan showing a house in relation to the property on which it stands

sleeper walls

walls that support the joists in a suspended timber type of ground floor

soakaway

a pit made in the subsoil some distance from the house, to which rainwater drains are connected

soffit board

a long board made of wood or asbestos sheet fixed under the eaves of a roof

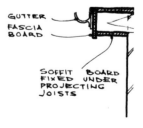

soil drain	a drain (i.e. a pipe below ground level) which conveys soil water, either alone or together with waste water or rainwater
soil pipe	a pipe above ground level which conveys soil water either alone or together with waste water or rainwater
soil and vent pipe	a single vertical pipe above ground level, the upper part of which is a ventilating pipe and the lower part a soil pipe
soil water	the effluent from a soil appliance (e.g. lavatory)
specification	a document describing in detail every item or operation which the builder is to price for in his quotation and carry out under his contract
stopping	filling in holes and splits in new wood
struts	in pitched roofs, timber pieces on which purlins are supported
studding	timber frame wall construction
surface water	rainwater drained from roofs or paved areas
tender	an offer to carry out certain work for a certain price under certain conditions; can be in the form of a special document
thermal insulation	method of reducing the loss of heat through a material or part of building
timber frame wall	a wall made of a framework of timber pieces to which boarding is nailed on each side

toe

the edge of a concrete foundation slab thickened to provide extra support

toothing

a method of joining a new to an existing wall: alternate courses of bricks project and fit into each other

trap

in drainage, a pre-formed section of a pipe or fitting designed to trap a small quantity of liquid which acts as a seal against odours returning or escaping from the drainage system

trussed rafter

triangular-shaped composite timber frame commonly used in the construction of a complete roof instead of separate timber rafters, joists and purlins; usually manufactured by specialist firms and delivered to a site ready for fixing into position

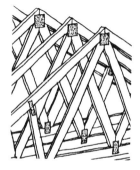

underpinning	the process of constructing new or more substantial foundations underneath an existing wall
unprotected area	any part of an external wall which does not have the prescribed degree of fire resistance, or any windows or other openings in the wall or any part of the wall with cladding of combustible material
vent pipe	a pipe open to the air at its highest point, for ventilation purposes only; does not convey any soil water, waste water or rainwater
wall ties	small strips of metal or wire used in a cavity wall to hold together the two leaves of the wall
waste water	water discharged from bath, basin, sink, shower, bidet (but not from a lavatory)
winders	tapered steps in a staircase turning a corner
wood-wool slabs	roofing slabs made of wood shavings and cement; they give good insulation
zone of open space	the prescribed amount of open space which has to be provided outside at least one window of a habitable room

air bricks, 107, gl.
arbitration, 90, 94
architect, 24, 32, 36, 50, 56, 61, 111
– as arbitrator, 94
– choosing, 9 *et seq*
– and contracts, 87
– and drawings, 75, 77
– fees, 11, 12
– services offered, 10, 11
– supervising builder, 98, 127
– and tenders, 95, 96
architectural consultant, 24, 32, 36,
   50, 56, 61, 94, 111
– choosing, 9 *et seq*
– and contracts, 87, 88, 90
– and drawings, 75, 77
– fees, 12
– and schedule of prices, 96
– services offered, 10, 12
– supervising builder, 98, 127

back-inlet gully, 104, 124, gl.
balanced flue, 59
barge boards, 115, gl.
bathroom extension, 50 *et seq*, 124
battens, 114, 115, 120, 121, gl.
bearing pressure, 105, gl.
bill of quantities, 96, gl.
binder, 62, 114, 115, gl.
block-bonding, 109, gl.
blocks
– breeze, 108, gl.
– clinker, gl.
– concrete, 31, 32, 71, 108, 109,110
borrowing, *see* finances
bricks, 31, 32, 71, 77, 108, 109, 110,
   123
builder, 24, 32, 111
– choosing, 13, 14
– on completion, 127, 128
– during construction, 98, 104 *et seq*
– and contract, 87 *et seq*, 127
– and drawings, 75, 77
– and estimates, 14, 16, 73, 95
– package deal firms, 14, 15
– and prefabricated units, 101, 102
– and quotations, 75, 95 *et seq*

building control office, 83, 128, 129
building control officer, 13, 24, 34, 46,
   83, 84, 85, 99, 104, 128
building line, 24, gl.
Building Regulations, 22 *et seq*
– approval, 75, 77, 82 *et seq*, 101
– relaxations, 83
building society, 2, 16
building surveyor, 24, 32, 36, 50, 56,
   61, 111
– as arbitrator, 94
– choosing, 9 *et seq*
– and contracts, 87, 90
– and drawings, 75, 77
– fees, 12
– services offered, 9, 10
– supervising builder, 98, 127
– and tenders, 95, 96
by-laws, 22, 55
– inner London, 84

car port, 35, 73
cavity walls, 31, 74, 110, gl.
ceiling, 117
– garage, 71
– height, 7, 36, 62, 74, 103
– insulation, 74, 113, 117
charges
– architectural, 11 *et seq*, 77
– builder's, 14, 101, 127
– for district surveyor, 85
– package deal firms, 15
cladding, 27, 32, gl.
cleaning eye, 123, 124, gl.
concrete strip foundation, 105
conservatory, 23, 38, 46, 48
construction notes, 77, gl.
constructional hearth, 57
consultant, *see* architectural
contract, 15, 87 *et seq*, 98
– and completion, 127
– and tenders, 95 *et seq*
contract price, 87, 91, 93, 127
converting
– bedroom to bathroom, 54, 55
– integral garage, 73, 74
– loft, 60 *et seq*

cross-section, 7, 77, gl
cubic content, 19, 34, 35

damp-proof course, 33, 106, 108, 121, gl.
damp-proof membrane, 33, 70, 74, 108, 119, 120, gl.
deck, roof, 36, 38, 113, 117
decorations, 93, 123
defects, 102, 127, 128
Department of the Environment
— and listed buildings, 21, 81
— and planning permission, 81
district surveyor, 84, 85
dormer window, 62, 63, gl.
doors, 42, 111
— and fire resistance, 27, 71
— garage, 72
— and ventilation, 48
double glazing, 111
double-seal cover, 104, 124, gl.
downpipes, *see* pipes
drains, 50 *et seq*, 104, 124, 125, gl.
— existing, 3, 5, 24, 50
in inner London, 85
— land, 104
— surface water, 40, 72
drawings, 10, 75, 76, 77, 101
— for Building Regulations, 83
— for planning permission, 79, 80
— and tenders, 95, 98

eaves, 113, 118, gl.
electrical fittings, 55, 56, 92, 125, 126
elevations, 75, gl.
estimates, 14, 16, 73, 95, gl.
extensions
— bathroom, 50 *et seq*
— garage, 70 *et seq*
— ground floor, 24 *et seq*, 102, 103
— prefabricated, 100 *et seq*
— two-storey, 7, 20, 25, 35
— upper floor, 34, 35

fascia board, 38, 113, 115, 119, gl.
Federation of Master Builders, 13
fees, *see* charges

finances, 16 *et seq*
fire precautions
— and lofts, 60, 64
— and roofs, 36, 38, 72, 117
— and walls, 26 *et seq*, 73, 121
fire resistance, 26 *et seq*, 103, 121, gl.
fire-resistant doors, 27
firring pieces, 113, gl.
flashing, 113, 114, 116, 117, gl.
floors
— coverings, 33, 77, 120, 121
— foundations, 106
— garage, 70, 71, 74
— in loft, 62, 64
— solid, 33, 119, 120
— suspended, 33, 106, 107, 121
fluctuations clause, 87, 89, 91
flue, 56 *et seq*, gl.
— balanced, 59, gl.
foundations, 25, 34, 105, 106
— for prefabricated unit, 101 *et seq*

gable-ended roof, 36, 37
gas appliances, 55, 56, 58, 59
garage, 20, 23, 38, 70 *et seq*
— integral, 73, 74
— prefabricated, 102
— and upper storey, 34
glass bricks, 30
glazing bars, 117, gl.
grants, house improvement, 17, 18, 50
gully, 5, 40, 104, 124, gl.
gutters, 38 *et seq*, 72, 113, 115, 119

habitable room, 23, 24, 36, 102, 103, gl.
— and access to bathroom, 52 *et seq*
— in loft, 62
— open space outside, 42 *et seq*
— and ventilation, 48 *et seq*
hardcore, 106, 120, gl.
heating installations, 56 *et seq*
heights
— ceiling, 7, 36, 62, 74, 103
— flue outlets, 58, 59
— of loft, 62
— for staircase, 65, 66
hopper, 39, gl.

Incorporated Association of Architects
& Surveyors, 10
inner London, 22, 84, 85
inspection chamber, 3, 5, 50, 52, 104,
124, 125, gl.
insulation
– sound, 33, 64
– thermal, 31, 35, 36, 38, 64, 70, 74,
103, 117, gl.
insurance, 89, 91, 128

joists, 112, gl.
– ceiling, 38, 62, 63, 114, 115
– floor, 34, 62, 64, 106, 121
– roof, 36, 113, 114, 117

kitchen
– and access to bathroom, 52, 53
– as habitable room, 24, 42
– ventilation to, 48, 50
– and zone of open space, 42, 46

ladder, retractable, 65, 69
larder, 48
lavatory, 50, gl.
– access to, 52, 53, 54
– and drains, 123 *et seq*
– ventilation to, 50
lintol, 42, gl.
listed buildings, 21, 81
local authority, 78
– and Building Regulations approval,
24, 75, 77, 82 *et seq*, 95
– and grants, 17, 18
– loans, 17, 18
– and planning permission, 20, 75, 77,
78 *et seq*, 95
– and rates, 78, 129
loft conversion, 1, 60 *et seq*
lump sum contract, 87, 88 *et seq*

manhole, *see* inspection chamber
metric conversions, 130, 131
mortgage, 1, 16, 17

National Federation of Building Trades
Employers, 13, 18

oil-burning appliances, 56 *et seq*
oversite, 106, 107, gl.

package deal firms, 15
parapet wall, 39, 72, 118, 119
partially exempted buildings, 23, 83
partition wall, 32, 105, gl.
PC sum, 90, 92, 93, 97, 125, 127, gl.
permitted development, 19, 20
piers, 35, 70, 71, 110, gl.
pipes, 3, 4, 5, 39, 51, 123, 124, 125
– flue, 56, 57, 59, 64, 125
– rainwater, 3, 39, 72, 102, 119, gl.
– soil, 3, 52, 104, 123, 124, gl.
– ventilation, 3, 52, 64, gl.
– waste, 3, 51, 123, 124
see also drains
planning authority, 20, 21, 25, 36, 77,
78 *et seq*
planning permission, 19 *et seq*, 101
– appeals, 81
– applying for, 75, 77, 78 *et seq*
plans, *see* drawings, sketch
plastering, 64, 74, 117, 121, 122, 123
plate, timber, 113, 114, 121, gl.
plumbing, 55, 56, 61, 77, 92, 125
prefabricated units, 100 *et seq*
– car ports, 73
– garages, 102
priming, 93, 122, gl.
professional advice, 9 *et seq*, 99, 130
see also architect, architectural consultant, building surveyor
provisional items, 90, 92, 93, 97, 127
purlins, 62, 114, 115, 117, gl.

quantity surveyor, 96, gl.
quotations, 75, 77, 88, 95 *et seq*, gl.

rafters, 61, 62, 114, 117, gl.
– trussed, 61, gl.
rainwater disposal, 38 *et seq*, 72, 102,
119
see also pipes
rates, 78, 129
rendering, 32, gl.
ridge piece, 114, gl.

roof, 36 *et seq*, 77, 111 *et seq*
– flat, 36, 38, 72, 113
– garage, 72
– lean-to, 36, 37, 38, 116
– and loft conversion, 61 *et seq*
– pitched, 36, 37, 38, 72, 114
– and rainwater disposal, 38 *et seq*
– translucent, 38, 46, 72, 103, 117
Royal Institute of British Architects, 9
– form of contract, 87
Royal Institution of Chartered Surveyors, 10

schedule of prices, 95, 97
Scotland, 78
screed, 120, gl.
sewer, public, 5, 40, 52
siting, 24 *et seq*
sketch plan, 2 *et seq*
slates, 36, 38, 72, 115
sleeper walls, 106, 121, gl.
soakaway, 40, 41, 72, 104, gl.
soffitt board, 113, 115, 118, gl.
soil appliance, 51
soil and vent pipe, 3, 4, 125, gl.
solicitor, 15, 88
solid fuel appliances, 56 *et seq*
specification, 77, 95, gl.
spiral staircase, 65, 66, 67
stage payments, 93, 99
staircase, 35, 65
– to loft, 60, 65 *et seq*
– safety precautions, 60, 68
struts, 61, 62, 63, 115, gl.
studding, *see* timber frame walls
subcontracting, 92, 94
surveyor, 10, 17
see also building surveyor, quantity
surveyor
suspended floor, 33, 106, 107, 121

tenders, 95 *et seq*, gl.
thermal insulation, *see* insulation
tiles, 36, 38, 72, 115
timber frame walls, 32, 64, 122, gl.
timber, treated, 116, 120, 121, 123
toothing, 109, gl.

trap, 123, gl.
trussed rafter, 61, gl.
two-storey extension, 7, 20, 25, 35

unprotected areas, 26 *et seq*, gl.
upper floor extension, 34 *et seq*

valuation officer, 79, 129
value added tax, 13, 14, 88, 93
variations, 89, 91, 93, 96, 99, 126,
127
ventilation, 48 *et seq*, 64, 71, 74
– and gas appliances, 58, 59
– and lavatories, 52
– mechanical, 50
– under floor, 107

wall plate, 112, 113, 114, 121, gl.
wall ties, 31, gl.
walls
– cavity, 31, 74, 108, 110, gl.
– fire precautions, 26 *et seq*, 73, 121
– foundations, 105
– garage, 71
– materials, 31, 32, 71, 109
– partition, 32, 105, gl.
– solid, 31, 32, 110
– surfaces, 121, 123
– and thermal insulation, 31, 103
– thickness, 2, 3, 31, 32, 71
– timber frame, 32, 64, 122, gl.
waste appliances, 51, 124
water butt, 41, 72
water supply, 55, 56
winders, 65, gl.
windows, 21, 42 *et seq*, 77, 111
– and fire precautions, 27, 30, 71
– in lofts, 62, 64
– open space outside, 42 *et seq*
– and ventilation, 48 *et seq*
wood-wool slabs, 36, 117, gl.

zone of open space, 42 *et seq*, 64, 71,
74, gl.

Central heating
helps you to choose central heating for your home, giving details of the equipment involved—boilers, radiators, heat emitters, thermostats and other controls, warm air units, ducting—and discussing the different fuels, the importance of insulation, and the installation.

The legal side of buying a house
explains the legal processes of buying an owner-occupied house with a registered title in England or Wales (not Scotland). It takes you step-by-step through a typical house purchase, and also deals with the legal side of selling a house.

Electricity supply and safety
explains in simple, practical terms what everyone should know about the electricity supply in his house—voltage, frequency, wiring, fuses, earthing, insulation—and the procedure for getting electricity laid on.

Wills and probate
is a book about wills and how to make them, and about the administration of an estate by executors without the help of a solicitor. One section deals with intestacy and its particular difficulties.

Owning a car
is written for the ignorant car owner/driver, and explains what is involved in buying a car (new or secondhand), running, repairing and maintaining it, and what can be done when it breaks down.

What to do when someone dies
covers the formalities that have to be observed after a death, and explains about doctors' certificates, the coroner, registering the death, arranging for burial or cremation, the funeral, claiming national insurance benefits.

Health for old age
sets out in plain language the minor and major physical changes that arise as people grow older, and the treatments available to relieve them. Advice is given about maintaining health, and about going to the doctor.

Avoiding back trouble
deals with causes of lower back trouble and gives hints on general care of the back and how to cope with an acute attack. It explains about specialist examination and treatment.

Care of the feet
describes the structure and growth of the feet, and advises how to look after them, including choosing suitable shoes. Common foot troubles and disorders are discussed, and the treatments available to relieve them.

Infertility
sets out what can and should happen in the systematic investigation of childlessness, explaining the medical and surgical treatment available.

Treatment and care in mental illness
deals briefly with the illnesses concerned and describes the help available from the local authority and voluntary organisations. It explains the medical treatment and deals with aftercare and community care.

Pregnancy month by month
goes in detail through what should happen when you are going to have a baby, mentioning some of the things that could go wrong and what can be done about them, and describing the available welfare services.

The newborn baby
concentrates primarily on health and welfare in the first few weeks after the baby is born, but also covers development in the following months. There is advice about when and from whom to seek help.

Getting a divorce
explains the procedure for getting a divorce in England or Wales and when making arrangements afterwards.

Having an operation
describes admission to hospital and what happens there and gives basic information about the more common operations.

How to sue in the county court
goes step by step through what is involved in taking a case to the county court without a solicitor, explaining the procedure and rules through the example of suing a shop that sold a faulty washing machine.

Coping with disablement
gives advice and information about many aids and techniques for carrying out everyday tasks, and where and how help can be sought.

Claiming on home, car and holiday insurance
explains the procedure for making a claim on an insurance policy, interpreting the technical jargon and identifying the people and problems you may come across.

Living through middle age
explains the normal physical changes at this stage of life, and the changes that can be avoided. The menopause is fully discussed, and so are sexual and psychological aspects of middle age for both men and women.

Dismissal, redundancy and job hunting
for anyone who has been unfairly dismissed or made redundant, explains about compensation and taking a case to an industrial tribunal. It describes how to claim unemployment benefit and advises on how to set about getting another job.

Outings and in-things for children
is packed with ideas on how to occupy 5 to 12-year-olds in the holidays—outdoor and indoor museums, zoos, farm and town trails, lighthouse visits—and where to find out what's on.

Where to live after retirement
discusses the points to consider when deciding whether to move or stay put, describing the alternatives that may be available, such as sheltered housing or a residential home.

CONSUMER PUBLICATIONS are available from Consumers' Association, Caxton Hill, Hertford, SG13 7LZ and from booksellers.